Local Social Services Boards

in North Carolina

KRISTI A. NICKODEM

The School of Government at the University of North Carolina at Chapel Hill works to improve the lives of North Carolinians by engaging in practical scholarship that helps public officials and citizens understand and improve state and local government. Established in 1931 as the Institute of Government, the School provides educational, advisory, and research services for state and local governments. The School of Government is also home to a nationally ranked Master of Public Administration program, the North Carolina Judicial College, and specialized centers focused on community and economic development, information technology, and environmental finance.

As the largest university-based local government training, advisory, and research organization in the United States, the School of Government offers up to 200 courses, webinars, and specialized conferences for more than 12,000 public officials each year. In addition, faculty members annually publish approximately 50 books, manuals, reports, articles, bulletins, and other print and online content related to state and local government. The School also produces the Daily Bulletin Online each day the General Assembly is in session, reporting on activities for members of the legislature and others who need to follow the course of legislation.

Operating support for the School of Government's programs and activities comes from many sources, including state appropriations, local government membership dues, private contributions, publication sales, course fees, and service contracts.

Visit sog.unc.edu or call 919.966.5381 for more information on the School's courses, publications, programs, and services.

Aimee N. Wall, DEAN
Jeffrey B. Welty, SENIOR ASSOCIATE DEAN FOR FACULTY AFFAIRS
Anita R. Brown-Graham, ASSOCIATE DEAN FOR STRATEGIC INITIATIVES
Willow S. Jacobson, ASSOCIATE DEAN FOR GRADUATE STUDIES
Kara A. Millonzi, ASSOCIATE DEAN FOR RESEARCH AND INNOVATION
Lauren G. Partin, SENIOR ASSOCIATE DEAN FOR ADMINISTRATION
Sonja Matanovic, ASSOCIATE DEAN FOR STRATEGIC COMMUNICATIONS
Jen Willis, ASSOCIATE DEAN FOR ADVANCEMENT AND PARTNERSHIPS

FACULTY

Whitney Afonso	Jacquelyn Greene	Kristi A. Nickodem
Gregory S. Allison	Timothy Heinle	David W. Owens
Lydian Altman	Margaret F. Henderson	Obed Pasha
Rebecca Badgett	Cheryl Daniels Howell	William C. Rivenbark
Maureen Berner	Joseph Hyde	Dale J. Roenigk
Frayda S. Bluestein	James L. Joyce	John Rubin
Kirk Boone	Robert P. Joyce	Jessica Smith
Mark F. Botts	Diane M. Juffras	Meredith Smith
Brittany LaDawn Bromell	Kimberly Kluth	Michael Smith
Peg Carlson	Kirsten Leloudis	Carl W. Stenberg III
Melanie Y. Crenshaw	Adam Lovelady	John B. Stephens
Connor Crews	James M. Markham	Charles Szypszak
Crista M. Cuccaro	Christopher B. McLaughlin	Shannon H. Tufts
Leisha DeHart-Davis	Jill D. Moore	Emily Turner
Shea Riggsbee Denning	Jonathan Q. Morgan	Amy Wade
Sara DePasquale	Ricardo S. Morse	Richard B. Whisnant
Kimalee Cottrell Dickerson	C. Tyler Mulligan	Teshanee T. Williams
Phil Dixon, Jr.	Kimberly L. Nelson	Kristina M. Wilson

Printed in the United States of America
27 26 25 24 23   1 2 3 4 5
ISBN 978-1-64238-078-1

Contents

Chapter 4

The Size, Composition, and Status of the Board of Social Services ... 29

Chapter 5

Appointment, Terms, and Removal of Social Services Board Members ... 35

Chapter 6

An Overview of the Powers and Duties of the County Board of Social Services ... 49

Chapter 10
The Budgeting Process for Departments of Social Services ... 99

Chapter 11
The Role of the Board of County Commissioners in Social Services ... 105

Chapter 12
Ethical Standards and Legal Prohibitions for Social Services Board Members ... 113

Chapter 13
Social Services Board Meetings and Procedures ... 125

Preface

Local Social Services Boards in North Carolina is intended to provide social services board members with the information that they need to perform their responsibilities lawfully and effectively. It may also be a useful reference for county social services directors, social services attorneys, county commissioners, county managers, and county attorneys.

This book is the first in a three-part series that will also include books for local boards of health and consolidated human services boards. For more School of Government resources regarding social services, public health, and consolidated human services, please visit the North Carolina Human Services Hub at https://humanservices.sog.unc.edu/.

Local Social Services Boards in North Carolina revises, updates, and expands John L. Saxon's *Handbook for County Social Services Boards*, which was published by the School of Government in 2009. I am indebted to Professor Saxon for his important and thoughtful scholarship, which paved the way for this book. Professor Saxon's *Handbook* has been used for over a decade as a vital resource for social services boards and directors.

I am particularly grateful to Aimee Wall for reviewing many chapters of this book and providing valuable feedback on the book's contents. I would like to thank many other School of Government faculty members, including Frayda Bluestein, Connor Crews, Bob Joyce, Diane Juffras, Phil Dixon Jr., Kirsten Leloudis, Jill Moore, and Kristina Wilson—as well as Dominick D'Erasmo, at the Office of State Human Resources—all of whom provided helpful review and commentary regarding certain chapters of this book.

I am also grateful to Aimee Wall and my faculty colleague Jill Moore for their contributions to the research and analysis regarding organization and governance options for human services agencies. During their tenure at the School of Government, Wall and Moore have written countless blog posts, bulletins, book chapters, and instructional materials regarding the organization and governance of North Carolina's social services and public health agencies.

Finally, I am thankful to the social services board members, county directors of social services, consolidated human services directors, social services employees, and social services attorneys that I have interacted with since joining the School of Government's faculty. The questions and feedback I have received from these individuals have also shaped the contents of this book.

I hope that this book will help social services board members provide thoughtful, informed governance to North Carolina's social services agencies. These agencies provide crucial, life-saving services to countless North Carolina residents each year. Good governance is essential to the continued flourishing and stability of these agencies in the years to come.

Kristi A. Nickodem
Robert W. Bradshaw Jr. Distinguished Term Assistant Professor of
    Public Law and Government
The University of North Carolina at Chapel Hill
June 2023

Commonly Used Abbreviations

ALJ	administrative law judge
APS	adult protective services
BOCC	board of county commissioners
CHS	consolidated human services
CHSA	consolidated human services agency
CPS	child protective services
DSS	department of social services
G.S.	North Carolina General Statutes
N.C.A.C.	North Carolina Administrative Code
NCDHHS	North Carolina Department of Health and Human Services
OAH	Office of Administrative Hearings
OSHR	Office of State Human Resources
SHRA	State Human Resources Act (Chapter 126 of the North Carolina General Statutes)
SHRC	State Human Resources Commission

Chapter 1

An Overview of Social Services Governance in North Carolina

Welcome! This book is intended to help you understand your role and responsibilities as a board member of a county social services agency. You will learn about the laws governing the work of social services boards, the powers and duties of a county board of social services, the services and programs offered by county social services agencies, and the role of the county director of social services.

Before diving into those topics, this chapter will introduce you to the different types of local social services agencies and governing boards allowed under North Carolina law.

Department of Social Services Governance in North Carolina

Each county department of social services in North Carolina is required to have a governing board.[1] The type of governing board varies based on what type of agency the county has established, as shown in Table 1.1.

An additional governance option is available for county departments of social services (DSSs) and consolidated human services agencies (CHSAs). A board of

Table 1.1. Social Services Agencies and Governing Boards

Agency	Governing Board
County department of social services	County board of social services
Consolidated human services agency	Consolidated human services board
Regional department of social services[a]	Regional board of social services

[a] As of March 2019, North Carolina counties have authority to voluntarily join together to create regional departments of social services. *See* G.S. 108A, §§ 15.7–15.10. However, to date, no counties have opted to create a regional department of social services.

county commissioners (BOCC) may directly assume the powers, responsibilities, and duties of a county board of social services or a consolidated human services (CHS) board.[2] By doing so, the BOCC abolishes the appointed board.[3] The county commissioners cannot abolish and assume the powers and duties of a governing board for a multicounty agency, such as a regional board of social services or a district board of health.[4]

County commissioner governance of social services agencies is discussed in more detail in Chapter 11.

Recent Changes to Options for Structuring and Governing County Agencies

In 2012, the North Carolina General Assembly enacted Session Law (S.L.) 2012-126, which provided counties with broader options regarding organization and governance of their social services and public health functions (described in Table 1.2). Specifically, this law

- allowed any BOCC (in a county with a county manager) to combine two or more county human services functions into a single CHSA;[5] and
- allowed any BOCC to directly assume the powers and duties of one or more of the governing boards responsible for overseeing a local human services agency (a county board of health, county board of social services, or consolidated human services board).[6]

Prior to this change in the law, only counties with a population of at least 425,000 could create a CHSA[7] or have the BOCC assume and exercise the powers and duties of a county social services board or a consolidated human services board.[8] In the years after S.L. 2012-126 was enacted, many of North Carolina's most populous counties opted to create CHSAs.[9]

Key Differences Between Organization and Governance Models

Table 1.3 shows a quick reference guide to key differences between various governance and organization models for social services. When looking at this chart, make sure to identify which type of organization and governance structure exists in your county.

Table 1.2. County Human Services Agency Organization and Governance Options Under S.L. 2012-126

	Organization	Governance
Option A: separate agencies with appointed governing boards	Human services agencies (such as a local health department and county DSS) remain separate.	Local appointed governing boards (county board of health and county board of social services) oversee the county's local human services agencies.
Option B: separate agencies with partial or full BOCC governance	Human services agencies (such as a local health department and county DSS) remain separate.	The BOCC directly assumes the powers and duties of one or more of the governing boards responsible for overseeing a local human services agency (county board of health and/or county board of social services).[a]
Option C: CHSA with appointed CHS governing board	The BOCC creates a CHSA by combining two or more human services functions, departments, or agencies.	The BOCC appoints a CHS board that serves as the CHSA's governing board.
Option D: CHSA with BOCC governance	The BOCC creates a CHSA by combining two or more human services functions, departments, or agencies.	The BOCC becomes the CHSA's governing board by directly assuming the powers and duties of the CHS board.

Note: BOCC = board of county commissioners, CHS = consolidated human services, CHSA = consolidated human services agency.

[a] In some counties, the BOCC governs all human services agencies, while in others, the BOCC has only assumed governance of one agency while leaving another under the control of a local governing board.

CHS Boards and Regional DSS Boards

This book primarily focuses on information that is relevant to governing boards for standalone, nonconsolidated county departments of social services (Options A and B on Table 1.2) but will occasionally mention consolidated agencies and their governing boards for purposes of comparing and contrasting key differences.

More information about the creation, composition, and governance of CHSAs is available in Chapter 16 of this book. A new book for members of consolidated human services boards (and county commissioners who have assumed the powers and duties of a consolidated human services board) is forthcoming from the School of Government.

To date, no North Carolina counties have opted to create a regional department of social services, so this book rarely discusses regional boards of social services. For more information about the law regarding regional departments of social services and their governing boards, please read Chapter 17 of this book.

Table 1.3. Local Social Services Organization and Governance Options at a Glance

Organization	Governing Board	Board Members Selected By[a]	Director Appointed By	Employees
County DSS	County board of social services	Appointment (3 or 5)	Board	Subject to SHRA
County DSS	BOCC	Election	BOCC	Subject to SHRA
CHSA	Appointed CHS board	Appointment (Up to 25)	County manager, with the advice and consent of the CHS board	SHRA optional
CHSA	BOCC[b]	Election	County manager, with the advice and consent of the BOCC	SHRA optional
Regional DSS	Regional board of social services	Appointment (12–18)	Board	Subject to SHRA

Note: SHRA = State Human Resources Act, BOCC = board of county commissioners, CHS = consolidated human services, CHSA = consolidated human services agency.

[a] Numbers in parentheses represent the number of members on each appointed board.

[b] An advisory committee for public health must be appointed if the CHSA includes public health. The requirement for a health advisory committee applies only to counties that abolish their health boards after January 1, 2012. This amounts to an exception for Mecklenburg County, which abolished its health boards (a county board of health and subsequently a CHS board) before that date.

Appendices

This book compares and contrasts a number of differences between county boards of social services, consolidated human services boards, and regional boards of social services. For tables comparing differences between these three types of boards at a glance, please see Appendix A.

This book will introduce many concepts and topics, often at a relatively high level. Appendix B recommends resources—including books, papers, websites, and blog posts—for readers who are interested in exploring certain topics in more depth.

Finally, this book also uses a number of abbreviations. See page xi for an explanation of commonly used abbreviations.

Notes

1. Chapter 108A, Section 1 of the North Carolina General Statutes (hereinafter G.S.).
2. G.S. 153A-77(a).
3. Under G.S. 153A, § 76(5)–(7), county commissioners are prohibited from abolishing and assuming the powers and duties of (*a*) an area mental health, developmental disabilities, and substance abuse services board; (*b*) a public health authority assigned the power, duties, and responsibilities to provide public health services as outlined in G.S. 130A-1.1.3; (*c*) a public hospital authority authorized to provide public health services under S.L. 1997-502.4; or (*d*) a public hospital as defined in G.S. 159-39(a). A clause at G.S. 153A-76(6) provides an exception for Mecklenburg County with respect to the abolishment of the area mental health, developmental disabilities, and substance abuse services board, as Mecklenburg County had already abolished this board prior to January 1, 2012.
4. G.S. 153A-76.
5. G.S. 153A-77(b)(3).
6. G.S. 153A-77(a).
7. Wake County and Mecklenburg County were the only counties that opted to create CHSAs prior to the enactment of S.L. 2012-126.
8. Mecklenburg County was the only county that elected this option prior to the enactment of S.L. 2012-126.
9. As of the time this book goes to print, the following thirty counties provide social services through CHSAs: Alexander, Bladen, Brunswick, Buncombe, Cabarrus, Carteret, Clay, Dare, Davie, Edgecombe, Forsyth, Gaston, Guilford, Haywood, Lee, Mecklenburg, Montgomery, Nash, New Hanover, Onslow, Pender, Polk, Richmond, Rockingham, Stanly, Swain, Union, Wake, Wayne, and Yadkin.

Chapter 2

Social Services in North Carolina

County social services boards in North Carolina function within a large and complex social services system. Board members need to have a basic knowledge of this system to understand the broader legal framework around the agencies they govern. This chapter will introduce you to the legal roles and responsibilities of North Carolina counties, North Carolina state government, and the federal government with respect to social services policy, administration, and funding.

What Are Social Services?

The term *social services* refers to a diverse mix of programs and services intended to help individuals and families in need. In some cases, social services address personal safety needs by providing protection to a child or adult who has been abused or neglected. In other cases, social services address financial needs, by connecting low-income individuals and families with programs that can help them buy food or pay for heat in the winter. Some of these services and programs are offered by local public agencies, including county departments of social services, consolidated human services agencies (CHSAs), and agencies serving senior citizens, veterans, or survivors of domestic violence. Private organizations, including nonprofits and religious institutions, also offer many social services programs in North Carolina communities.

This book will focus primarily on the services and programs traditionally administered by county social service agencies in North Carolina. The terms *county social services agency*, *county department of social services*, and *county DSS* are used in this book to refer to the agency that carries out a county's obligations to provide social services and administer public assistance programs. In some counties, the county social services agency will be a CHSA. In areas where there are differences between a county DSS and a CHSA, the book will note those differences accordingly.

Social Services Programs and Agencies

Social services programs and agencies address a range of economic and social problems that impair the ability of individuals to function and thrive in society. These problems include poverty, hunger and food insecurity, lack of medical care, homelessness and unstable housing, child abuse and neglect, abuse and neglect of vulnerable adults, and unemployment. Such problems affect the general well-being and stability of society as a whole, not just the individuals and families experiencing them directly. When county social services agencies address these problems, they are making an investment in the long-term flourishing and stability of the community.

North Carolina counties are required by state law to provide certain social services within their jurisdictions. Many counties also offer additional services tailored to community needs. Each county social services agency administers dozens of social services programs, and each of these programs has its own rules regarding eligibility, assistance, services, administration, and funding. The services and programs provided by a county DSS can be divided into two primary categories: economic services and social work services.

Economic services, also referred to as public assistance programs, assist eligible people through monetary payments and other economic supports. This category includes programs such as Food and Nutrition Services, Medicaid, and Low-Income Energy Assistance. Most economic services programs are *means-tested*, meaning that eligibility is determined based on a person's or family's income and resources.[1]

Social work services, on the other hand, are typically provided without regard to income. Social work services provided by a county social services agency include protecting children and vulnerable adults who are at risk of abuse or neglect, acting as a public guardian to individuals adjudicated incompetent by a court, and helping families navigate the licensing process for foster care and adoption. Table 2.1 lists some examples of programs that are means-tested and some that are not.

Overview of North Carolina's Social Services System

North Carolina has adopted a county-administered, state-supervised social services system under which social services programs are *administered* primarily by county agencies under the *supervision* of various state-level entities.[2] North Carolina is one of only a small number of states in which social services programs are directly administered by counties rather than the state.[3] In most states, the state directly administers social services programs through a centralized administrative system.[4] This means that in most states, local governments have "little or no role in administering or financing state and federal social services programs."[5] North Carolina's unique model has implications for counties related to funding, governance, liability, staff, and program administration.

Each county social services agency exists at a complex intersection of federal, state, and county involvement with the agency's funding, policy, and operations.

Table 2.1. Examples of Social Services Programs

Means-Tested	Not Means-Tested
Food and Nutrition Services	Child protective services
Medicaid	Adult protective services
Work First (Temporary Assistance for Needy Families)	Public guardianship
Child Care Subsidy	Child support enforcement

Federal Involvement

The federal government funds many of the programs offered by county DSS agencies and attaches specific requirements to the administration of those programs. That federal funding is received by the state, which in turn allocates that funding to the counties.

State Involvement

The state is responsible for ensuring that counties comply with applicable federal and state law related to mandated social services programs, as well as allocating state funding to counties and establishing policies for county agencies.

County Involvement

Each North Carolina county is responsible for establishing a social services agency, determining a governance structure for the agency, hiring and supervising social services staff, funding part of the cost of social services programs, and administering social services programs in compliance with state and federal law.

The unique roles of federal, state, and county government in North Carolina's social services system are described in more detail in the following sections of this chapter.

The Federal Government's Role and Responsibilities

Federal law does not require any state to operate particular social services programs. Rather, Congress appropriates funds available to states that agree to operate certain social services programs in accordance with applicable federal law. In other words, the federal government provides funding to states that choose to operate certain programs, but that funding comes with strings (legal requirements) attached.

The level of federal financial participation varies from program to program. With respect to the costs of programs that involve federal or state financial participation or both—that is, excluding programs funded only by counties—the North Carolina

Department of Health and Human Services (NCDHHS) estimates that for state fiscal year 2023–2024, federal funds will provide

- over 93 percent of the direct costs of public assistance programs;
- over 64 percent of associated administrative costs for public assistance programs; and
- over 56 percent of the costs of services programs.[6]

Though the federal government does not require states to provide particular social services programs, the federal government offers significant financial incentives for states to make federally supported social services programs available to their residents.[7]

The federal executive agency with primary responsibility for overseeing most social services programs is the U.S. Department of Health and Human Services. The U.S. Department of Agriculture oversees food and nutrition programs. These agencies promulgate regulations to carry out federal laws, issue policies to the states, and monitor state compliance with federal requirements. They can impose financial sanctions on states for failing to meet these requirements. Federal laws and regulations may dictate many different aspects of program administration, including eligibility, benefit amounts, duration of assistance or services, and confidentiality of program information.

There is no direct relationship between the federal government and counties with respect to federally funded social services programs. The federal government provides funding for these programs to each state and holds the *state* accountable for complying with federal requirements and conditions. However, counties are still required to comply with the federal laws associated with these programs, because the federal mandates that are imposed on the state are passed on to counties along with federal funding for social services programs.[8]

The State's Role and Responsibilities

The North Carolina Constitution recognizes the state's duty to provide "beneficent provision for the poor, the unfortunate, and the orphan"[9] and requires the state to establish and operate "such charitable [and] benevolent . . . institutions and agencies as the needs of humanity and the public good may require" in a manner to be determined by the North Carolina General Assembly.[10]

The North Carolina General Assembly

The General Assembly is primarily responsible for determining the extent and scope of the state's responsibility for social services and how the state will discharge that responsibility. The General Assembly has enacted laws that require counties to carry out a substantial portion of the state's responsibility for social services.[11]

Among other things, laws enacted by the General Assembly

- authorize the state to participate in federal-state social services programs;[12]
- designate NCDHHS as the single state agency responsible for supervising the administration of federal-state social services programs;[13]
- appropriate state funding for social services programs;
- allocate federal social services funds received by the state;
- establish the role, authority, and responsibility of county governments with respect to social services; and
- determine how the state and counties will share responsibility for the nonfederal portion of the cost of federally supported programs.[14]

Much of the social services legislation enacted by the General Assembly is codified in Chapter 108A of the North Carolina General Statutes, which includes laws regarding county administration of social services programs, confidentiality of social services records, and financing of social services programs.[15] However, many details regarding the funding, administration, and supervision of social services programs do not appear in the General Statutes. Some are addressed by administrative rules and policies promulgated by NCDHHS and the state Social Services Commission, while others are decided by the General Assembly when it appropriates funds for public assistance and social services programs.[16]

The North Carolina Department of Health and Human Services

NCDHHS is the state agency that is responsible for supervising the administration of state and federal-state social services programs.[17] This includes issuing policies for use by county social services agencies in interpreting and implementing the various laws and regulations governing social services programs. NCDHHS also handles some administrative functions directly or through contracts with private vendors, such as processing and paying Medicaid claims, operating the child support enforcement program in certain counties, making medical determinations for Social Security and state Medicaid Disability claims, and hearing administrative appeals involving eligibility for certain social services programs.

In addition to creating policies and providing technical assistance, NCDHHS also has the authority to take corrective action in the event that a county social services agency is noncompliant with the law.[18] Each county department of social services is required to enter into an annual written *memorandum of agreement* with NCDHHS (sometimes referred to as a memorandum of understanding, or MOU) that sets out specific performance requirements and administrative responsibilities for all mandated social services programs, with the exception of Medicaid.[19] When a county social services agency fails to comply with the terms of the written agreement, the mandated performance measures, or other applicable laws, NCDHHS has the authority to provide technical assistance, create and implement a corrective action plan, divest the county director of social services of service delivery powers, and ultimately control county service delivery directly or through a contract with a public or private agency.[20] If NCDHHS determines that a county social services agency is not providing child protective services, foster care services, or adoption services in accordance with state law and regulations, NCDHHS may act on an emergency basis to temporarily take over the delivery of child welfare services in that county, and may withhold state and federal funding for child welfare services from the county.[21]

State Commissions

Three state commissions play a significant role in the state's social services programs: the Social Services Commission, the Child Care Commission, and the State Human Resources Commission. These commissions adopt regulations found in the North Carolina Administrative Code, which have the force and effect of law.

Social Services Commission

This commission has broad authority to adopt rules that govern most of the state's social services programs.[22] The commission is also authorized to establish standards for inspecting and licensing maternity homes, adult care homes for aged or disabled persons, and residential child care facilities. The commission may authorize investigations of social problems, subpoena witnesses, and compel the production of documents.[23] In counties having an appointed board of social services, the Social Services Commission appoints either one or two members (depending on whether the county has a three- or five-member board).[24] The governor appoints the commission's members, one from each congressional district, for four-year terms.[25]

Child Care Commission

This commission adopts standards and rules for the licensing and operation of child care facilities.[26] It also is charged with making rules for responding to child abuse or neglect in child care facilities.[27] The commission has seventeen members—nine appointed by the governor and eight by the General Assembly—that serve for two-year terms.[28]

State Human Resources Commission

This commission, in conjunction with the Office of State Human Resources, establishes policies and rules related to many aspects of the State Human Resources Act (SHRA).[29] All employees of a (nonconsolidated) county DSS are subject to the SHRA and to the State Human Resources Commission's rules for local government employees.[30] The commission has nine members—four appointed by the General Assembly and five by the state governor—that serve for four-year terms.[31]

The Counties' Roles and Responsibilities

As discussed above, North Carolina is an outlier in the national social services landscape because of the amount of responsibility placed on counties for the funding and administration of social services programs. The role of counties with respect to social services in North Carolina is based on state laws that authorize or require counties to administer or fund social services programs and require counties to establish social services agencies and governing boards.[32]

Under North Carolina's state-supervised and county-administered system, county social services agencies are primarily responsible for administering social services programs, under the supervision of NCDHHS.[33] Under this system, county social services agencies are part of county government, and employees of county social services agencies are county employees. In addition, North Carolina counties must pay part of the administrative costs associated with social services programs and part of the cost of the direct assistance and services provided under many social services programs.

For instance, NCDHHS estimates that for state fiscal year 2023–2024, county funds will provide

- 2.17 percent of the direct costs of public assistance programs;
- 35.68 percent of associated administrative costs for public assistance programs; and
- 38.61 percent of the costs of social services programs (such as child protective services, adult protective services, and child support enforcement).[34]

More information about the county's role in financing social services programs may be found in Chapter 10.

North Carolina's unique social services system reflects the state's long history of county responsibility for social services. It provides counties with a high level of flexibility and control over the structure, governance, and internal operations of their social services agencies. However, the state-supervised, county-administered nature of North Carolina's social services system continues to generate concerns among some stakeholders, as evidenced by ongoing debates regarding intercounty collaboration, county funding obligations, information sharing between counties, child welfare reform, and the nature of state supervision over county operations.[35]

As shown in Table 2.2, North Carolina counties have a substantial amount of responsibility for the administration and funding of social services programs. The powers and duties of county commissioners, county social services agencies, directors of social services, and social services governing boards are defined by and subject to state law and state supervision. In some instances, these powers and duties are also constrained by federal law, including federal confidentiality laws and federal requirements attached to funding for social services programs.

Each board of county commissioners is responsible for establishing an agency to provide social services and choosing a governance structure for that agency.[36]

Table 2.2. Division of State and County Responsibility for Social Services in North Carolina

State	County
• Accept federal funding for social services programs; transmit federal and state funding to counties	• Allocate county funding to social services agency; pay county's share of nonfederal costs for federally funded programs
• Develop state law and policy	• Administer programs locally in compliance with federal and state laws and state policy
• Provide oversight and supervision of county-level administration of social services programs	• Hire, train, and supervise local staff to administer and deliver social services programs
• Provide technical assistance to county agencies	• Determine agency structure and governance model

Counties have several different options regarding the type of agency that will provide social services in the county and the type of board that will govern that agency. The agency and governance structure a county chooses will affect the hiring process for the agency director and agency staff, who are all recruited and hired at the local level.

Organization

A county has three options for organizing the local agency that delivers social services. The county may

- operate a county department of social services,
- establish a CHSA that includes social services,[37] or
- establish a regional (multicounty) department of social services.[38]

More information about CHSAs is available in Chapter 16. More information about regional departments of social services is available in Chapter 17. As of the publication of this book, no North Carolina counties have opted to create a regional department of social services.

Governing Board

State law requires every county in North Carolina to have a governing board for social services, which may be

- an appointed county board of social services,
- a consolidated human services (CHS) board,
- a regional board of social services, or
- a board of county commissioners that exercises the powers and duties of a county board of social services or a CHS board.[39]

The governance options available to each county depend in part on the organizational model that the county has chosen for providing social services. For more information about how the organization and governance options fit together, refer to Chapter 1.

Director

Regardless of the type of organization that administers social services programs in a county, someone must be appointed to serve in the role of director of social services.[40] The director administers the public assistance and social services programs directly and through the social services staff.[41] The person or entity with authority to appoint the director differs based on the agency structure a county has in place.

In a county with a county DSS, the *social services board* must appoint a director of social services for the DSS.[42]

In a county with a CHSA, the *county manager* must appoint a CHS director, who in turn assumes all of the powers and duties of a social services director.[43] The CHS director may delegate some or all of these social services powers and duties to another employee (sometimes called the "DSS director"), but the CHS director retains the ultimate responsibility for ensuring that all obligations and functions involving social services programs and policies are carried out.[44]

If counties form a regional department of social services, the *regional board of social services* must appoint a regional director of social services for the department.[45]

Staff

Employees of a county DSS or a CHSA are county employees. Different rules and policies may apply to social services agency employees based on the agency structure a county has in place.

- In a county DSS or regional DSS, the agency's employees are hired by the DSS director and are subject to the SHRA and certain State Human Resources Commission rules.[46]
- In a CHSA, the agency's employees are hired by the CHS director with the approval of the county manager.[47] When creating a CHSA, county commissioners can choose to keep the CHSA's employees subject to the SHRA or can opt to remove them from the coverage of the SHRA and make them subject solely to county personnel policies and procedures.[48]

For more information on the role of a board of county commissioners in choosing a county's organization and governance model for social services, funding social services programs, making decisions regarding social services programs, appointing a special attorney for social services matters, and approving the salary for the county DSS director, please see Chapter 11 of this book.

Notes

1. The federal poverty guidelines (sometimes called the "federal poverty level") provide one important measure for determining whether an individual or family qualifies for means-tested services. The federal poverty guidelines are established by the U.S. Department of Health and Human Services. They are adjusted each year, vary based on the number of persons in the household, and attempt to provide a rough measure of the income a family needs to obtain adequate housing, food, and other necessities. In 2022, the federal poverty guideline for a family of three living in North Carolina was $23,030 per year. Various social services programs have different rules regarding whether and how the federal poverty guidelines are used to determine eligibility for services.

2. John L. Saxon, Social Services in North Carolina, 5 (UNC School of Government, 2008).

3. For example, the majority of states have state-administered child welfare programs. Only nine states can be described as county-administered: California, Colorado, Minnesota, New York, North Carolina, North Dakota, Ohio, Pennsylvania, and Virginia. Two "hybrid" states, Nevada and Wisconsin, are partially administered by the state and partially administered by counties. *State vs. County Administration of Child Welfare Services*, Child Welfare Info. Gateway (2018), https://www.childwelfare.gov/pubs/factsheets/services/.

4. N.C. Gen. Assembly, Program Evaluation Div., Statutory Changes Will Promote County Flexibility in Social Services Administration, Rep. No. 2011-03 (May 2011), https://www.ncleg.net/PED/Reports/documents/DSS/DSS_Report.pdf.

5. *Id.* at 3.

6. N.C. Dep't of Health & Hum. Servs., *County Budget Estimates State Totals—State Fiscal Year 2023–2024*, https://www.ncdhhs.gov/divisions/social-services/county-staff-information/budget-information/dss-budget-estimates (scroll to the heading County Budget Estimates 2023-2024 and select Budget Estimates State Totals to access PDF).

7. *See* Aimee N. Wall, *Social Services*, *in* County and Municipal Government in North Carolina ch. 39 (Frayda S. Bluestein ed., UNC School of Government, 2d ed. 2014).

8. Saxon, *supra* note 2, at 41.

9. N.C. Const. art. XI, § 4.

10. N.C. Const. art. XI, § 3.

11. *See* Martin v. Bd. of Comm'rs, 208 N.C. 354 (1935) (care of indigent sick and afflicted poor is a proper function of state government, but the General Assembly may require counties, as administrative agencies of the state, to perform this function within their territorial limits); Bd. of Managers of James Walker Mem'l Hosp. v. City of Wilmington, 237 N.C. 179 (1953); Craven Cnty. Hosp. Corp. v. Lenoir Cnty., 75 N.C. App. 453 (1985).

12. *See* Chapter 108A, Section 71 of the North Carolina General Statutes (hereinafter G.S.).

13. G.S. 108A-71.

14. For example, for many years the state and counties shared responsibility for paying for the nonfederal share of the cost of Medicaid services. In 2007, the General Assembly enacted legislation that ultimately phased out the county's share for Medicaid services but still requires counties to help pay for costs of administering the program (S.L. 2007-323, § 31; S.L. 2007-345, § 14). Another example is found in G.S. 108A-49.1, which provides that the nonfederal share of foster care and adoption assistance payments will be divided equally between the state and county.

15. Other laws regarding social services agencies, employees, and programs are codified in G.S. Chapters 7B (Juvenile Code), 48 (Adoptions), 110 (Child Welfare), 126 (State Human Resources Act), and 153A (Counties).

16. Wall, *supra* note 7, 667–68. Some social services policy decisions are included in uncodified session laws, such as uncodified provisions of the state's biennial appropriations act, which specifies who is eligible for Medicaid and what services will be provided under the state's Medicaid program. The state's biennial appropriations act also allocates federal funding received by the state under the Social Services Block Grant, the TANF Block Grant, the Child Care and Development Block Grant, and the Low-Income Energy Assistance Block Grant, and it appropriates money from the state's General Fund for social services agencies and programs.

17. G.S. 108A-71; G.S. 143B, art. 3.

18. G.S. 108A-74 (authorizing NCDHHS to take various remedial measures when a county or a regional social services agency fails to comply with its mandated performance requirements or applicable law, ranging from a corrective action plan to an NCDHHS takeover of the agency, in which the director of social services is divested of service delivery powers).

19. *Id.* G.S. 108A-74 also sets forth the procedures for NCDHHS intervention, including notice requirements.

20. G.S. 108A, § 74(a)–(c).

21. G.S. 108A-74(h).

22. G.S. 143B, art. 3, pt. 6. The secretary of NCDHHS, rather than the Social Services Commission, has rulemaking authority for the Medicaid program.

23. G.S. 143B-153.

24. G.S. 108A-3.

25. G.S. 143B-154.

26. G.S. 143B-168.3.

27. G.S. 110-88.

28. G.S. 143B-168.4.

29. G.S. 126-4. Prior to 2013, the Office of State Human Resources was named the Office of State Personnel and the commission was named the State Personnel Commission. S.L. 2013-382.

30. *See* G.S. 126 (State Human Resources Act); Subchapter 1I of Title 25 of the North Carolina Administrative Code. Even though the director and staff of county social services departments are county employees, their employment is governed by the SHRA unless (1) the county's personnel system, or a portion of it, has been approved by the State Human Resources Commission as being "substantially equivalent" to the SHRA or (2) the county has incorporated the social services department into a consolidated human services agency and elected to remove the agency's employees from the SHRA.

31. G.S. 126-2.

32. North Carolina counties are political subdivisions of the state and may exercise only those powers conferred on them by state law.

33. *See* G.S. 108A, §§ 1, 14(3), 25.

34. *See* N.C. Dep't of Health & Hum. Servs., *supra* note 6. These estimated totals group together many different programs, which may receive highly differing levels of county funding (for example, adult services often receive much lower county funding than child welfare services).

35. For more information on these issues, see, e.g., CTR. FOR THE SUPPORT OF HEALTHY FAMS., SOCIAL SERVICES REFORM PLAN (May 6, 2019), https://www.osbm.nc.gov/documents/files/socialservicesreform-finalplan/download; SOC. SERVS. REG'L SUPERVISION & COLLABORATION WORKING GRP., STAGE ONE FINAL REPORT (UNC School of Government, March 2018); and SOC. SERVS. REG'L SUPERVISION & COLLABORATION

Working Grp., Stage Two Final Report (UNC School of Government, December 2018). Both of the working group's final reports are available at https://www.sog.unc.edu/resources/microsites/social-services/reports.

36. *See* G.S. 108A-1.
37. This option is only available to counties with a county manager. *See* G.S. 153A-77(b).
38. *See* G.S. 108A-15.7 (regional departments of social services).
39. G.S. 108A-1.
40. G.S. 108A-12.
41. G.S. 108A-14.
42. *Id.*
43. G.S. 153A-77(e); G.S. 108A-15.1(c). The county manager's decision to appoint the director must be made with the advice and consent of the CHSA's governing board (which may be an appointed CHS board or the BOCC).
44. For more information on delegation of authority within a CHSA, please see Kristi A. Nickodem, *Personnel Decisions for North Carolina's Consolidated Human Services Agencies*, Soc. Servs. Bull. No. 49 (UNC School of Government, 2021).
45. G.S. 108A-15.8(a).
46. G.S. 108A, §§ 14(a)(2), 15.10; G.S. 126-5(a)(2).
47. G.S. 153A-77(e).
48. G.S. 153A-77(d). To date, the majority of counties that have created CHSAs have opted to remove employees from the coverage of the SHRA, in favor of making them subject solely to county personnel policies and procedures. For more information on this decision regarding SHRA coverage, please see Kristi A. Nickodem, *supra* note 44.

Chapter 3

Social Services Agencies, Programs, and Services

North Carolina counties have several options for structuring the local agency that will provide social services programs. This chapter will introduce you to the three different types of local social services agencies and the programs and services these agencies provide to the public.

Types of Local Social Services Agencies

North Carolina counties may choose to provide social services programs through a county DSS, a consolidated human services agency (CHSA) that includes social services, or a regional (multicounty) department of social services.[1] As of the time this book goes to print, thirty counties provide social services through a CHSA and seventy counties provide social services through a county DSS. To date, no North Carolina counties have opted to create a regional department of social services. Table 3.1 shows some key differences between these agency-organization models.

What are the most significant differences between the agency structures described in Table 3.1?

- A CHSA is the only organizational structure in which the county manager, rather than the agency's governing board, has the authority to appoint, supervise, and dismiss the agency director. However, the county manager's appointment and dismissal decisions must be made with the advice and consent of the CHSA's governing board.
- A CHSA is the only organizational model for social services in which social services employees may be exempt from the State Human Resources Act (SHRA).[2]
- A regional department of social services is the only organizational option that allows multiple counties to join together to form a single department.

Table 3.1. Options for Organization of Local Social Services Agencies

	County DSS	CHSA	Regional DSS
Structure	Single county	Single county	Multicounty
Governance options[a]	Appointed county board of social services (3 or 5) or BOCC	Appointed CHS board (up to 25) or BOCC[b]	Appointed regional board of social services (12–18)
Employees subject to	SHRA	County personnel policies unless county opts in to SHRA	SHRA
Director appointed by	Governing board[c]	County manager, with advice and consent of governing board[c]	Governing board

Note: CHS = consolidated human services, CHSA = consolidated human services agency, BOCC = board of county commissioners, SHRA = State Human Resources Act.
[a] Numbers in parentheses represent the number of members on each appointed board.
[b] Advisory committee must be appointed if CHSA includes public health.
[c] This governing board may be a BOCC.

More information about CHSAs is available in Chapter 16 of this book. More information about regional departments of social services is available in Chapter 17. For information on how county commissioners can change the structure of a county's social services agency, please see Chapter 11.

The terms *county social services agency*, *county department of social services*, and *county DSS* are used in this book to refer to the agency that carries out a county's obligations to provide social services and administer public assistance programs. In some counties, the county social services agency will be a CHSA. In areas where there are differences between a county DSS and a CHSA, the book will note those differences accordingly.

Facilities for Social Services Agencies

Each county is required to provide adequate physical facilities for the offices of the county's social services agency. All facilities occupied by county social services agencies must meet certain state standards with respect to the types and amount of office space, privacy, accessibility, and storage. These state standards (found in Title 10A, Chapter 67A, Section .0103 of the North Carolina Administrative Code) include, among other things,

- private offices for the county director and each supervisor, and
- private offices or interviewing rooms available to all staff who interview clients.

Employees of Social Services Agencies

County Departments of Social Services

All employees of county social services agencies are county employees. However, unlike most other county employees, employees of a county DSS are subject to most of the provisions of the SHRA, which includes requirements regarding hiring, classification, promotion, compensation, and dismissal of employees.[3]

In counties with a county manager, the manager is responsible for hiring and firing the employees of most county departments.[4] This is not true, however, with respect to employees of the county DSS. Instead, state law gives the county DSS director the exclusive authority to hire, supervise, and discipline county DSS employees.[5] Even in the absence of a permanent full-time director, the social services governing board has no authority to hire DSS personnel.[6]

Given that DSS employees are generally subject to the SHRA and State Human Resources Commission rules, what role does the county play? State law authorizes boards of county commissioners to adjust the salary ranges for positions subject to the SHRA (including DSS employees and the DSS director) so that the ranges will conform to local financial ability and fiscal policy.[7] These adjustments are subject to approval by the State Human Resources Commission.[8] State law also allows the board of county commissioners to enact personnel ordinances regarding annual leave, sick leave, hours of work, holidays, and the administration of the pay plan for county employees, which will apply to county social services employees if those county rules and regulations are filed with the director of the Office of State Human Resources.[9] In addition, the board of county commissioners effectively determines the number of county DSS employees through its approval of the county DSS budget.

Consolidated Human Services Agencies

For a county with a CHSA, the CHSA's employees are subject to *county* personnel ordinances and policies unless the board of county commissioners explicitly chooses to keep them subject to the SHRA's requirements.[10] Most counties in North Carolina that have created CHSAs have opted to make CHSA employees subject solely to county personnel ordinances and policies instead of the SHRA.[11] Unlike a county DSS director, a CHSA director's hiring decisions are subject to the county manager's approval.[12]

Programs and Services Offered by Social Services Agencies

State law requires counties to administer or assist in the administration of a number of social services and economic services programs, including

- Medicaid,[13]
- Health Choice for Children,[14]
- Work First,[15]
- Food and Nutrition Services,[16]

- Low-Income Energy Assistance,[17]
- State-County Special Assistance,[18]
- Foster Care and Adoption Assistance,[19]
- child protective services,[20]
- adult protective services,[21]
- guardianship services,[22] and
- child support enforcement services.[23]

If a county identifies a need in the community that is not addressed by these programs, state law authorizes each county to undertake, sponsor, organize, engage in, and support any other social services program that will further the health, welfare, education, employment, safety, comfort, and convenience of its citizens.[24]

Several of the largest programs provided by county social services agencies are described below. However, this list is by no means exhaustive.[25]

Food and Nutrition Services

State law requires every county to operate the federally funded Supplemental Nutrition Assistance Program (SNAP), known in North Carolina as the Food and Nutrition Services (FNS) program.[26] This was previously referred to as the "food stamp" program. Through this program, counties issue electronic-benefit-transfer (debit) cards to eligible recipients for the purchase of food products.[27] Eligibility is based on federal income and resource guidelines. The federal government pays the full cost of SNAP benefits. The federal government also pays half of the administrative costs for the program, while in North Carolina, counties pay the other half.[28] In December 2022, the state reported that there were over 819,900 active cases in this program, providing assistance to more than 1.6 million individuals.[29]

Medicaid

Medicaid is a public assistance program that covers most of the cost of medical care and services for several categories of people who cannot afford these costs.[30] Those who may receive Medicaid include low-income aged, disabled, or blind persons; needy children; pregnant women; individuals who receive federal Supplemental Security Income benefits; and others with low incomes who meet eligibility requirements. In state fiscal year 2022, the federal government provided 69.1 percent of North Carolina's Medicaid funding, while the state contributed 30.9 percent of the program's total funds.[31] Over 2.8 million individuals in North Carolina were eligible for Medicaid in state fiscal year 2022.[32]

Work First

The federal Temporary Assistance for Needy Families (TANF) program is called "Work First" in North Carolina.[33] The federal government provides a set amount of TANF funding (a *block grant*) to each state to implement programs intended to support families who are in need.[34] Work First focuses on providing eligible families with short-term assistance to help them achieve self-sufficiency through employ-ment.[35] The program provides cash assistance as well as assistance with child care, transportation, job searches, and job training. In December 2022, the state estimated that this program was providing cash assistance to over 18,000 individuals.[36]

Counties must notify NCDHHS as to whether they desire to be designated as either "electing" or "standard" counties for purposes of administering the Work First program.[37] The General Assembly makes these designations based on recom-mendations from NCDHHS.[38]

- In an electing county, the board of county commissioners is responsible for development, administration, and implementation of the Work First program in the county.[39]
- In a standard county, the county social services agency is responsible for administering and implementing the Standard Work First program (which is established, developed, and monitored by NCDHHS) in the county.[40]

Chapter 11 contains more information regarding the differences between standard and electing counties with respect to Work First.

Other Public Assistance Programs

Social services agencies are also involved with administering other public assistance programs, such as the Child Care Subsidy Program, the Low-Income Energy Assis-tance Program (LIEAP), the State-County Special Assistance for Adults Program, the Foster Care and Adoption Assistance Programs, and the Refugee Assistance Program (RAP).

Child Support Enforcement Program

The Child Support Enforcement program assists parents in establishing and enforc-ing child support obligations, including locating absent parents for the purpose of obtaining child support and establishing paternity of dependent children.[41] In most counties the program is administered by the county DSS or a CHSA, but in some counties it is administered by another department of county government or by a contracted provider.[42] Child support agencies must seek support on behalf of depen-dent children who receive public assistance through certain programs and must also provide services to anyone else who applies and pays a low application fee.[43]

Protective Services for Children

State law requires that cases of suspected child abuse, neglect, dependency, and death from maltreatment be reported to a county social services agency.[44] The North Carolina Juvenile Code, which includes this reporting requirement, is designed to protect children under age 18 from neglect and abuse by parents or other caretak-ers.[45] The Juvenile Code also requires that protective services be provided for any child who either has no parent or caretaker or whose parent is unable to care for the child or make suitable alternative arrangements.[46] When a county social services agency receives a report, it must conduct a prompt assessment and take appropriate action to protect the child.[47] Each agency provides a wide range of supportive services to children and their families in these cases, often while the children remain in the home, since one purpose of the law is to keep families intact unless the risk of harm to a child requires the child's removal from the home.[48] When necessary, a county social services agency may file a petition in district court seeking either legal custody of a child or some other court order to protect the child.[49]

Permanency Planning Services

Permanency planning services are provided by every county social services agency to children who are separated from their parents or caretakers and are in agency custody.[50] The goal of permanency planning services is to provide all children with permanent homes, preferably with their own families of origin, as early as possible. While the emphasis is on preserving or reunifying families, there is a complementary focus on moving children into long-term plans like adoption or guardianship when returning them to their own homes is not possible.

Adoptions

Adoption placement services are designed to find safe and permanent homes for children whose parents have relinquished them for adoption or had their parental rights terminated. Every county social services agency has an adoption program that includes accepting children for placement, recruiting and screening adoptive parents, and arranging and supervising placements.[51] State adoption law requires that either a county social services agency or a licensed child-placing agency conduct a preplacement assessment of every prospective adoptive home and report to the court on almost every adoptive placement.[52] The state Division of Social Services supervises county adoption programs and provides resources for families interested in adoption.

Protective Services for Adults

Each county social services agency is charged with receiving and responding to reports regarding the abuse, neglect, or exploitation of disabled adults.[53] When a county social services agency receives a report, it must conduct a prompt assessment and take appropriate action to protect the vulnerable adult.[54] In some cases, the agency may need to petition the district court for an order authorizing the provision of protective services to the vulnerable adult.[55]

Services to Aged or Disabled Adults

In addition to the protective services described above, county social services agencies provide a number of services to older adults and adults with disabilities that include in-home services, community-based services, and institutional care. Some of these services are mandatory, while others are optional.[56] An example of a mandated service is the agency's duty to conduct regular inspections of adult care homes to ensure their compliance with state licensing requirements and other state laws and regulations concerning the care and treatment of elderly or disabled residents.[57] An example of an optional service is the operation of an adult day care program, which is a supervised program offered to individuals with cognitive or physical impairments to promote their social, physical, and emotional well-being.[58] While some services and programs are provided by a county social services agency, some jurisdictions have created separate departments of aging and adult services or offer services through another county department.

Other Programs and Services

County social services agencies provide many programs and services that are not described in this chapter. It is important for members of the governing board for a county social services agency to take a proactive role in researching and understanding the unique social services programs administered by the agency they help to govern.

The Role of the Board with Respect to Social Services Programs

State law authorizes county social services boards to establish policies for certain social services programs.[59] Practically speaking, that authority is quite limited, as described in Chapter 9 of this book. Nonetheless, understanding what these programs do, whom they serve, and how they are funded is essential to understanding the role of the social services agency in the community.

Notes

1. *See* G.S. 108A-15.7 (regional departments of social services); G.S. 153A-77 (CHSAs). The option to create a CHSA is only available to counties with a county manager. *See* G.S. 153A-77(b).
2. When creating a CHSA, the BOCC has the option to keep CHSA employees subject to the SHRA but is not required to do so. *See* G.S. 153A-77(d).
3. G.S. 126-5(a)(2). Counties can exempt county DSS employees from certain aspects of the SHRA through receiving a designation from the State Human Resources Commission that the county's personnel system is "substantially equivalent" to the SHRA's standards in particular areas. G.S. 126-11(a); 25 N.C.A.C., 01I, § .2407.
4. G.S. 153A-82(a).
5. G.S. 108A-14(a)(2); *In re* Appeal of Brunswick Cnty., 81 N.C. App. 391 (1986).
6. *In re* Appeal of Brunswick Cnty., 81 N.C. App. at 397.
7. G.S. 126-9(b); *see also* 25 N.C.A.C. 01I, §§ .2101–.2103, .2106–.2107.
8. G.S. 126-9(b); *see also* 25 N.C.A.C. 01I, §§ .2101–.2102, .2107.
9. G.S. 126-9(a); G.S. 153A-94.
10. G.S. 153A-77(d); *see also Personnel Decisions for North Carolina's Consolidated Human Services Agencies*, SOC. SERVS. L. BULL. NO. 49 (UNC School of Government, Dec. 2021).
11. Some counties may not have personnel ordinances, in which case the CHSA employees would be subject to whatever policies the county has in place for county employees.
12. G.S. 153A-77(e)(1).
13. G.S. 108A-25(b).
14. G.S. 108A, §§ 70.26(a), 70.20.
15. G.S. 108A-27(f), (g).
16. G.S. 108A, §§ 25(a)(3), 51.
17. G.S. 108A-25(a)(5).
18. G.S. 108A, §§ 25(a)(2), 40.
19. G.S. 108A-25(a)(4).
20. G.S. 7B-302.
21. G.S. 108A-103.
22. G.S. 108A-15.
23. G.S. 110-141.
24. G.S. 153A-255. For examples of some potential limitations on this authority, see *Hughey v. Cloninger*, 297 N.C. 86 (1979) and *Stam v. State*, 302 N.C. 357 (1981).
25. The author is grateful to Aimee Wall for her descriptions of social services programs, upon which this section is based. *See* Wall, *Social Services, in* COUNTY AND MUNICIPAL GOVERNMENT IN NORTH CAROLINA ch. 39 (Frayda S. Bluestein ed., UNC School of Government, 2d ed. 2014). For a more detailed discussion of services and programs, see JOHN L. SAXON, SOCIAL SERVICES IN NORTH CAROLINA (UNC School of Government, 2009), 161–201.
26. G.S. 108A-51.
27. G.S. 108A, §§ 51–53.
28. *See* N.C. Dep't of Health & Hum. Servs., *County Budget Estimates State Totals—State Fiscal Year 2022–2023*, https://www.ncdhhs.gov/divisions/social-services/county-staff-information/budget-information/dss-budget-estimates (under the heading County Budget Estimates 2022-2023, select Budget Estimates State Totals to access PDF).

29. *See* N.C. Dep't of Health & Hum. Servs., *FNS Caseload Statistics Reports: FNS Cases and Participants*, https://www.ncdhhs.gov/divisions/social-services/program-statistics-and-reviews/fns-caseload-statistics-reports (click the link FNS Cases and Participants to download Excel file).

30. G.S. 108A, §§ 54–70.16.

31. *See* N.C. Dep't of Health & Hum. Servs., *State Fiscal Year 2022 Medicaid Annual Report Tables*, https://medicaid.ncdhhs.gov/reports/annual-reports-and-tables.

32. *See Id.*

33. G.S. 108A-25(b1).

34. 42 U.S.C. § 601.

35. G.S. 108A-27.

36. *See* N.C. Dep't of Health & Hum. Servs., *Work First Caseload Statistics: Work First Cash Assistance and Participants*, https://www.ncdhhs.gov/divisions/social-services/program-statistics-and-reviews/work-first-caseload-statistics (click the link Work First Cash Assistance Cases and Participants to download Excel file).

37. G.S. 108A-27(e). When notifying NCDHHS of the county's desire to be designated as electing or standard, the county must submit documentation demonstrating that three-fifths of its county commissioners support the desired designation.

38. G.S. 108A, § 27.2(12)–(14).

39. G.S. 108A-27(f). Electing counties must develop biennial Work First plans and submit them to NCDHHS for approval. *See* G.S. 108A, §§ 27.3(a)(12), 27.4(a).

40. G.S. 108A, §§ 27(g), 27.8(a).

41. G.S. 110, art. 9.

42. *See* G.S. 110-141 (requiring all counties to administer a child support enforcement program).

43. *See* G.S. 110-130.1; 42 U.S.C. §§ 608(a)(2), 654(29); 42 C.F.R. § 433.145–.148.

44. G.S. 7B-301.

45. G.S. 7B, subch. I.

46. G.S. 7B, §§ 101(9), 300.

47. G.S. 7B-302.

48. G.S. 7B-100.

49. G.S. 7B, art. 5.

50. N.C. Div. of Soc. Servs., *Permanency Planning Services Policy, Protocol, and Guidance, in* NC Child Welfare Manual (updated Sept. 2022), https://policies.ncdhhs.gov/divisional/social-services/child-welfare/policy-manuals/permanency-planning_manual.pdf.

51. G.S. 108A, § 14(a)(6), (13).

52. G.S. 48-1-109; *see generally* G.S. 48.

53. G.S. 108A, §§ 14, 15. "Disabled adult," the term used in the reporting statute, means any person 18 years of age or over or any lawfully emancipated minor who is present in North Carolina "and who is physically or mentally incapacitated due to an intellectual disability, cerebral palsy, epilepsy or autism; organic brain damage caused by advanced age or other physical degeneration . . . or due to conditions incurred at any age which are the result of accident, organic brain damage, mental or physical illness, or continued consumption or absorption of substances." G.S. 108A-101.

54. G.S. 108A, §§ 103–106.

55. G.S. 108A, §§ 104–106.

56. Local governments, both cities and counties, have the authority to "undertake programs for the assistance and care of senior citizens" but are not required to do so. G.S. 160A-497.

57. G.S. 131D-2.11(b); *see also* 10A N.C.A.C. 13F, § .1212.

58. *See* N.C. Div. of Aging & Adult Servs., Adult Day Care and Adult Day Health Services Procedures Manual (updated Jan. 2020), https://www.ncdhhs.gov/v35-3-3-2020-adc-adhs-policy-procedure-manual-2/open; *see also* 10A N.C.A.C. 06P, § .0502.

59. G.S. 108A-1.

Chapter 4

The Size, Composition, and Status of the Board of Social Services

State law requires every county in North Carolina to have a governing board for social services.[1] In addition to providing guidance to the local social services agency's director, the governing board for social services is charged with advising local government officials with respect to the development of policies and plans to improve social conditions in the community.[2]

Depending on the organizational model that the county has chosen for providing social services, the governing board for social services could be

- an appointed county board of social services,
- a consolidated human services (CHS) board,
- a regional board of social services, or
- a board of county commissioners (BOCC) that exercises the powers and duties of a county board of social services or a CHS board.[3]

Table 4.1 shows how these different types of governing boards correspond with different organizational structures, as well as key distinctions with respect to size of the board, appointment of the board, and appointment authority over the agency's director.

Information about the role, size, composition, and status of CHS boards is available in Chapter 16. Information about these topics for regional boards of social services is available in Chapter 17.

The remainder of this chapter will discuss the size, composition, and legal status of appointed county boards of social services governing county departments of social services.

Table 4.1. Types of Local Governing Boards for Social Services

Governing Board	Agency	Board Members Selected By[a]
Appointed county board of social services	County DSS	Appointment (3 or 5)
BOCC as board of social services	County DSS	Election
Appointed CHS board	CHSA	Appointment (Up to 25)
BOCC as CHS board[b]	CHSA	Election
Regional board of social services	Regional DSS (multicounty)	Appointment (12–18)

Note: BOCC = board of county commissioners, CHS = consolidated human services, CHSA = consolidated human services agency.

[a] Numbers in parentheses represent the number of members on each appointed board.

[b] An advisory committee for public health must be appointed if CHSA includes public health. G.S. 153A-77(a). There is no corresponding requirement to appoint an advisory committee for social services, though the BOCC may choose to do so.

Size and Composition

Appointed county social services boards may consist of either three or five members.[4] Before 1963 almost all county social services boards consisted of three members. Today almost all North Carolina counties with appointed county social services boards have five-member boards, while only a few counties have three-member boards.

If a county has a three-member board of social services, the board of county commissioners may increase the size of the social services board to five members.[5] State law also allows the BOCC to decrease the size of the county social services board from five to three members.[6] The commissioners' action to decrease (or increase) the size of the social services board is not subject to approval by NCDHHS, the state Social Services Commission, the county social services board, or the county DSS director. However, the decision to increase or decrease the size of the board must be reported immediately in writing by the chair of the BOCC to NCDHHS.[7]

State law does not require that a county social services board include a county commissioner.[8] However, BOCCs often choose to appoint at least one county commissioner to serve on their counties' social services boards.

The Role of the Director in Relation to the Board

The county social services director is the board's executive officer and acts as the board's secretary.[9] The social services director, however, is not a member of the county social services board. This means that the director may not vote as a board member or vote to break a tie vote by the board. It also means that the board is not required to allow the director to attend a closed session of the board, though it may choose to do so. For more information on conducting board business in closed session, please see Chapter 13 of this book.

Legal Status of County Social Services Boards and Board Members

County social services boards are not political subdivisions, departments, agencies, or units of state government.[10] Instead, county social services boards are local government boards that are part of North Carolina's system of county government. They are subject to state laws that apply specifically to county boards of social services[11] and to state statutes that apply generally to local government boards, such as North Carolina's open meetings law[12] and public records law.[13] More information about some of those laws is available in Chapters 12, 13, and 14 of this book.

Members of county social services boards are appointed local government officials, meaning they are subject to the provisions of the North Carolina Constitution and state statutes governing appointed local government officials. For example, the North Carolina Constitution and state laws require public office holders, including social services board members, to take and subscribe an oath of office (described in more detail in Chapter 5).[14]

Board of County Commissioners as the Governing Board for Social Services

A board of county commissioners has authority under state law to directly assume the powers and duties of a county board of social services.[15] A BOCC that wishes to assume the powers and duties of a local board must hold a public hearing after providing thirty days' notice of the hearing and intended action, and then adopt a resolution formally assuming the powers and duties of the board.[16]

When a BOCC assumes the powers and duties of a county board of social services, the existing county board of social services is dissolved and abolished. A BOCC then acquires all of the county board of social services' responsibilities, including the authority to appoint, evaluate, discipline, and dismiss the director of social services.

More information about county commissioner governance of social services agencies is available in Chapter 11 of this book.

The North Carolina Association of County Boards of Social Services

The North Carolina Association of County Boards of Social Services (NCACBSS) is a nonprofit organization that seeks to inform, educate, and empower county social services board members. NCACBSS's mission also includes advocating for the interests of county boards of social services, county departments of social services, and the employees and clients of county departments of social services. NCACBSS publishes a newsletter, maintains a website,[17] and helps plan statewide training programs for county social services board members.

The association is governed by a board of directors elected by NCACBSS's members, including six officers and fifteen regional directors. NCACBSS's annual business meeting generally is held in conjunction with the Social Services Institute, an annual conference that is sponsored by the North Carolina Association of County Directors of Social Services.

Membership in NCACBSS is open to (1) any member of a county board of social services (including members of a CHS board or a BOCC that has assumed the powers and duties of a social services board); (2) any member of a human services advisory committee to a BOCC that has assumed the powers and duties of a social services board; and (3) any person who has previously served as a member of a county board of social services and is continuously involved in programs affiliated with NCACBSS. Information about NCACBSS membership dues may be found in Article III of the NCACBSS by-laws, which are available on the NCACBSS website.[18]

Notes

1. Chapter 108A, Section 1 of the North Carolina General Statutes (hereinafter G.S.).
2. With respect to CHS boards, the law contemplates that the board will advise local officials "through the county manager." G.S. 153A-77(d).
3. G.S. 108A-1.
4. G.S. 108A-2.
5. G.S. 108A-5(b). If the BOCC expands the social services board from three to five members, the BOCC appoints one additional social services board member for a term that expires at the same time as the term of the incumbent social services board member who was appointed by the state Social Services Commission. The Commission appoints an additional social services board member for a term that expires at the same time as the term of the incumbent social services board member who was appointed by the BOCC. The expansion of the social services board becomes effective when both of the additional board members have been appointed.
6. G.S. 108A-5(c). A resolution decreasing the size of the social services board from five to three members becomes effective on the first day of July following adoption of the resolution and abolishes (1) the seat held by the board member appointed by the state Social Services Commission whose term would have expired on June 30, 2025 (or triennially thereafter) and (2) the seat held by the board member appointed by the BOCC whose term would have expired on June 30, 2023 (or triennially thereafter).
7. G.S. 108A-2.
8. G.S. 108A-3 specifically states that the BOCC may appoint "a county commissioner or a citizen." Compare with G.S. 153A-77(c) (requiring a CHS board to include a county commissioner).
9. G.S. 108A-14(a)(1).
10. *See* Meyer v. Walls, 347 N.C. 97 (1997).
11. These laws are primarily found in G.S. 108A.
12. G.S. 143, art. 33C.
13. G.S. 132.
14. N.C. Const. art. VI, § 7; G.S. 153A-26; G.S. 11-7.
15. *See* G.S. 153A-77. The BOCC cannot abolish and assume the powers and duties of a district board of health, a public health authority board, or a regional board of social services. G.S. 153A-76.
16. G.S. 153A-77. The notice of said public hearing must be "given in a newspaper having general circulation in [the] county."
17. The NCACBSS website may be found at http://www.ncacbss.org/.
18. N.C. Ass'n of Cnty. Bds. of Soc. Servs., NCACBSS By-Laws pp. 1–2 (Oct. 2015), http://www.ncacbss.org/By-Laws_October_2015.pdf.

Chapter 5

Appointment, Terms, and Removal of Social Services Board Members

This chapter will discuss legal issues related to the appointment, terms, and removal of members of an *appointed county board of social services.* Appointment, terms, and removal issues for members of the consolidated human services board are discussed in Chapter 16. These issues are discussed in Chapter 17 for members of a regional board of social services.

Legal Authority to Appoint Board Members

On a three-member county social services board, one member is appointed by the state Social Services Commission, one member is appointed by the board of county commissioners (BOCC), and one member is appointed by the majority of the other county social services board members.[1] On a five-member board, two members are appointed by the state Social Services Commission, two by the BOCC, and one by the majority of the other county social services board members.[2] If the members are deadlocked in their decision to appoint a third or fifth board member, the county's senior resident superior court judge appoints this third or fifth board member.[3] Table 5.1 shows the appointment authority for each appointing body.

Schedule for Board Terms and Making Appointments

Regular appointments to the county social services board are made on a staggered, three-year schedule that is linked to the dates on which the terms of county social services board members begin and end, as shown in Table 5.2. A "regular" appointment is any appointment other than (1) one that is made to fill the unexpired term of

Table 5.1. Appointment Authority for County Social Services Boards

	No. of Members Appointed	
Appointing Body	Three-Member Board	Five-Member Board
Board of county commissioners	1	2
Social Services Commission	1	2
Members of the county social services board	1[a]	1[a]

[a] If the board is deadlocked, the county's senior resident superior court judge appoints this member.

a board member who has resigned, died, or been removed from the board or (2) one that is made when the size of the social services board is being increased from three to five members.

Term Length

The term of a county social services board member lasts for three years and ends on June 30.[4] Regular appointments (or reappointments) to the county social services board should be made shortly before the expiration of an incumbent board member's term on June 30 or as soon as possible thereafter.

If an appointing authority fails to make an appointment to the social services board before the end of an incumbent board member's term or a newly appointed board member has not assumed office as of July 1, the incumbent board member continues to hold office as a "holdover" member after June 30 until the incumbent's successor is appointed *and* takes the oath of office.[5] A subsequent section of this chapter discusses the requirement to take the oath of office.

The regular term of a county commissioner who is appointed to the county social services board is three years, just like all other social services board members, and is not tied to or affected by the individual's tenure or term as a county commissioner.[6]

Term Limits

State law provides that a person generally may not serve more than two consecutive three-year terms on the county social services board.[7] Terms are consecutive when a subsequent term begins *immediately* after the expiration of a prior term.

There is a special exception for some board members who are county commissioners. The two-consecutive-term limit does not apply to a social services board member who (1) was a county commissioner at any time during the member's first

Table 5.2. County Board of Social Services Terms and Appointment Schedule

Term Period[a]	Appointing Bodies (Board Member Order No.)	
	Three-Member Board	Five-Member Board
July 1, 2022–June 30, 2025 (and triennially thereafter)	BOCC (1)	BOCC (1) SSC (4)
July 1, 2023–June 30, 2026 (and triennially thereafter)	SSC (2)	SSC (2) BOCC (5)
July 1, 2021–June 30, 2024 (and triennially thereafter)	Other social services board members (3)	Majority of social services board members (3)

Note: Dates and order of appointment are derived from G.S. 108A-5.
BOCC = board of county commissioners, SSC = Social Services Commission.
[a] Terms last three years each, running from July 1 of the first year to June 30 of the third.

two consecutive terms on the social services board and (2) is a county commissioner at the time the member is reappointed to the social services board.[8]

Another special exception applies when individuals serve partial terms on the board because they are appointed to fill a vacancy caused by the death, resignation, or removal of a board member. When a social services board member is appointed to serve the remainder of an unexpired term of a former board member, the unexpired term does not count toward the two-consecutive-term limit.[9]

Theoretically, any social services board member could serve an additional (third) term on the social services board so long as the term did not *immediately* follow the first two consecutive terms. How long must a former board member wait before becoming eligible for reappointment? State law does not answer that question. A cautious approach is to require board members who have served two consecutive terms to wait for the length of a full term (three years) before they can be reappointed to the board.

Appointments to Fill Vacancies and Partial Terms

Appointments to fill vacancies on the social services board caused by the death, resignation, or removal of a board member before the end of the board member's term must be made by the appointing authority that appointed the board member who left the seat vacant.[10] For example, if a county social services board member appointed by the Social Services Commission resigned in the middle of serving a term, the Social Services Commission would have the sole authority to appoint someone to fill that vacancy. Likewise, if a board member appointed by the county commissioners resigned during a term on the social services board, the BOCC would have the sole authority to fill that vacancy.

The term of a board member who is appointed to fill a vacancy on the social services board resulting from the death, resignation, or removal of another board member is a *partial* term, not a regular three-year term. The partial term begins on the date that the new board member assumes office following the new board member's appointment and ends on the date that the term of the new board member's predecessor in office would have expired.[11] In other words, the new social services board member appointed to fill the vacancy completes the unexpired remainder of the former board member's term on the board rather than serving a new full three-year term.

As described earlier in this chapter, when a social services board member is appointed to serve the remainder of an unexpired term of a former board member, the unexpired term does not count toward the two-consecutive-term limit.[12] An individual could be appointed to fill a vacancy on the board for a partial term and then go on to be appointed to two consecutive regular (three-year) terms immediately following the expiration of the partial term.

Qualifications for Appointment

Individuals are not required to have any specific professional or personal experience to be appointed to the county social services board. The only express legal qualification for appointment to the county social services board is that the appointee be a bona fide resident of the county at the time of appointment.[13]

State law does not specify what it means to be a "bona fide resident[]" for purposes of meeting this requirement. This concept is likely equivalent to "legal residence" or "domicile," which requires actual residence in the county, a present intent to make that county home, and a lack of present intent to reside in a different county.[14] State law does not require a prospective appointee to reside in a county for any minimum period of time before being appointed to the social services board.

State law does not provide any authority for county social services boards, the Social Services Commission, or NCDHHS to establish additional legal qualifications for county social services board members. However, boards of county commissioners do have authority to establish additional qualifications for members of the county board of social services as long as those additional qualifications are not inconsistent with state law and do not waive any state-law requirements.[15] For example, state law does not require the BOCC to appoint a commissioner to the social services board, but a BOCC could choose to require that one of its appointees to the social services board must always be a commissioner. As an alternative example, a BOCC could require that one of its appointees to the social services board must be a current or former recipient of social services.

Evaluating Potential Appointees

Each appointing authority—the Social Services Commission, the BOCC, and the members of the social services board—must exercise its own independent discretion and judgment when choosing social services board members. Accordingly, each appointing entity may want to develop its own process for screening and evaluating potential appointees out of a pool of county residents who are willing to serve on the social services board. Social services board members have authority to make significant decisions regarding the county DSS director—decisions that can substantially affect the county DSS, county employees, and county residents. In some circumstances, social services board members will have access to confidential social services information (see Chapter 9). In light of these responsibilities, appointing authorities should act carefully when selecting individuals to serve on a social services board.

Though county residency is the only legal qualification for serving on the board, appointing authorities may want to gather and evaluate additional information about prospective appointees for purposes of selecting between qualified individuals interested in board service. For example, an appointing authority may want to ask questions of potential appointees regarding why they are interested in serving on the board, whether they have any relevant professional or volunteer experience, and whether they have any current or past experience serving on any other state or local government boards, commissions, or committees.

Legal Disqualifications to Appointment

North Carolina law establishes only three express disqualifications that prevent the appointment of certain individuals to a county social services board.[16]

Multiple Office-Holding

North Carolina's laws that limit multiple office-holding disqualify a person from serving on the county social services board if, at the time the appointee would assume the board seat, the appointee already holds

- two appointive public offices or
- one elective public office and one appointive public office.[17]

This prohibition does not apply to a county commissioner who is appointed to the social services board by the BOCC (an *ex officio* appointment).[18] Ex officio appointments are discussed in more detail in Chapter 11.

Term Limits

A person is not eligible to be reappointed to the county social services board if that person is an incumbent board member, has served two consecutive three-year terms on the board, and is not a county commissioner who is exempt from the two-consecutive-term limit. As described earlier in this chapter, a board member may eventually be eligible for reappointment after a meaningful waiting period following the two consecutive terms, but the length of that waiting period is not defined by state law.

Prior Conduct in Public Office

The North Carolina Constitution disqualifies a person from holding any public office, including the office of county social services board member, if the person has been removed from any public office by impeachment or has been found guilty of corruption or malpractice in any public office.[19]

Other Considerations

While there are only three express disqualifications that legally prohibit a person from serving on the county social services board, there are certainly other reasons that might cause an appointing authority, in the exercise of its discretion and judgment, to decide that a particular person should not be appointed to the county social services board.

Although the fact that an individual has been convicted of a crime may be considered in determining whether the individual should be appointed to the county social services board, the fact that an individual has been convicted of a felony does not legally disqualify the individual from being appointed to the social services board if the individual's citizenship rights (such as the right to vote, hold public office, and sit on a jury) have been restored.[20]

Conflicts of Interest That May Limit Board Service

As a general matter, the fact that an individual or the individual's spouse, child, parent, sibling, or other close relative is receiving or has received public assistance or social services from the county social services department does not legally prohibit that individual from being appointed to the social services board or from continued service on the social services board. To the contrary, the experience of receiving public assistance or social services may help inform a board member's service on the board and provide a valuable perspective to other board members.

However, there are a couple of unique conflicts of interest related to public assistance and social services that may limit an individual's ability to serve on the social services board.

Payment for Adult Care or Nursing-Home Residents

State law expressly prohibits a county social services board member or the board member's spouse from receiving payments under the State-County Special Assistance or Medicaid programs on behalf of persons who are residents or patients in adult care or nursing homes that are owned or operated, in whole or in part, by the board member or the board member's spouse.[21] This law does not prohibit an individual who owns an adult care or nursing home (or someone whose spouse owns such a facility) from serving on the social services board, but it does effectively cut off an important source of revenue for these individuals in a way that might preclude them from serving on the board.

Foster Parents for the County

County social services board members are prohibited from (1) being licensed as foster parents through the social services department of the county in which they serve on the social services board or (2) being supervised or considered as a placement resource by the social services department of the county in which they serve on the social services board.[22]

The Appointment Process

All discussions and actions by the Social Services Commission, boards of county commissioners, and county social services boards regarding the appointment of county social services board members must take place in an open session of an official, public meeting of the appointing authority, in accordance with North Carolina's open meetings law.[23]

Although the open meetings law allows a public body to hold a closed session to discuss or take action with respect to some matters, appointments to the county social services board may not be considered or made during a closed session.[24] The open meetings law also prohibits the appointment of social services board members by "secret ballot." Each member of the appointing authority who votes on the appointment of a county social services board member must do so by voice vote, show of hands, or signed ballot (and if signed ballots are used, each member's vote must be announced when the ballots are counted and the minutes of the meeting must show the vote of each voting member).[25] The open meetings law is discussed in more detail in Chapter 13 of this book.

Appointments by the Social Services Commission or County Commissioners

Appointments to the county social services board by the Social Services Commission and boards of county commissioners must be approved by a majority vote of the commissioners who are present at an official meeting at which a quorum is present.

For the Social Services Commission, a majority of the Commission's members constitutes a quorum.[26] For boards of county commissioners, a majority of the board's membership, without regard to vacancies, constitutes a quorum.[27] For example, if a board of county commissioners has six members, four members must be present to have a quorum, even if a seat becomes vacant.[28]

Appointments by the Majority of the County Social Services Board Members

The appointment of a county social services board member by the majority of the four (or two) social services board members appointed by the Social Services Commission and the board of county commissioners requires

- a unanimous vote by both of the other board members on a three-member board or
- a vote of at least three of the other four board members on a five-member board.[29]

An incumbent social services board member who was appointed to the board by the other social services board members (or by the senior resident superior court judge) may not vote with respect to the member's own reappointment or the selection of the member's successor but may participate in the board's deliberations (unless prohibited from doing so under the board's own rules of procedure).

State law does not specify the procedure through which the senior resident superior court judge should be asked to appoint a county social services board member when a majority of the other social services board members are unable to agree with respect to the appointment. State law does not set forth any procedure for the judge to make the appointment, nor does it require the judge to hold a public hearing on the appointment, to make findings of fact or explain the basis for the decision, or to enter a judicial order making the appointment.

Procedural Issues Regarding Appointments

Except as limited by state law, each appointing authority may develop its own procedure and policies regarding the recruitment, nomination, and appointment of social services board members. The state Social Services Commission, for example, has adopted a nominating form for requesting that the Commission appoint an individual to a county's social services board.

As a best practice, an appointing authority's policies and procedures regarding the recruitment, nomination, and appointment of social services board members should

- be in writing, have been validly adopted by the appointing authority, and be publicly accessible;
- indicate the means for identifying potential nominees;
- indicate the procedures and time frames for making and accepting nominations;
- allow sufficient time for soliciting and considering nominations;
- specify the qualifications for appointment and identify what is expected of appointees; and

- ensure that all potential appointees are qualified, are able and willing to serve if appointed, and understand the role and responsibilities of county social services board members.

The county DSS director has no authority or responsibility with respect to recruiting, nominating, or appointing members of the county social services board. However, state law does not prohibit the director from providing assistance, making recommendations, or offering nominations to an appointing authority with respect to social services board appointments. If the director is involved in recruiting or nominating social services board members, that involvement should be handled in a way that does not compromise the appointing authority's independent judgment and discretion.

Oath of Office Following Appointment

As public officials, county social services board members are required to take an oath in which they swear or affirm that they will faithfully discharge the duties of their office and will support and maintain the constitutions and laws of the United States and North Carolina.[30] Board members should take this oath prior to assuming office.[31] The oath may be taken at any time between the date when an individual is appointed to the board and the date when the individual assumes office as a social services board member. Newly appointed social services board members often take their oaths of office at the first board meeting following the beginning of their terms.

The oath of office may be administered anywhere within the state by a judge, magistrate, clerk of superior court, state legislator, county or city clerk, mayor, chair of a BOCC, notary public, or other public official described in Chapter 11, Section 7.1 of the North Carolina General Statutes.[32] A written copy of the oath signed by a newly appointed social services board member must be filed with the clerk of the BOCC.[33]

If a county social services board member is reappointed for a second consecutive term, the board member should take a new oath of office and file a signed copy of the oath with the clerk of the BOCC. A county commissioner who is appointed by the BOCC to serve on the county social services board is not required to take a separate oath of office as a social services board member.

If an official who is required to take the oath fails to do so, there can be serious consequences. It is a misdemeanor to enter upon the duties of a public office without first taking, subscribing, and filing "the oath of office prescribed."[34] A public official who fails to take the oath of office may also incur a $500 penalty and ejectment from office.[35]

Revoking or Rescinding Appointments

State law does not allow an appointing entity to revoke or rescind an appointment after the appointing entity has taken action to appoint a person to the county social services board. However, board members may be removed from office for "good cause," as described below.[36]

Removal of Social Services Board Members

Legal authority to remove a social services board member from office is vested in the commission, board, or public officials who appointed the board member (the appointing authority).[37] For example, a social services board member who was appointed by the Social Services Commission may be removed from office only by the Social Services Commission, while a board member appointed by a BOCC may be removed only by the BOCC.

North Carolina law is silent with respect to specific grounds and procedures for removal of county social services board members from office during their terms. By contrast, it provides specific grounds and procedures for removal of consolidated human services board members and members of county boards of health.[38]

State law does provide several grounds for removal of *any* public official, which would apply to social services board members.

1. A public official is subject to being ejected from office for failure to take the oath of office prior to assuming the duties of the office.[39]
2. A public official may be removed from office for willful failure to discharge the duties of the office.[40]
3. A public official who holds office in a manner that is contrary to article VI, section 9 of the North Carolina Constitution "forfeit[s] all rights . . . incident thereto."[41] This would include someone who violates the prohibition on multiple office-holding described earlier in this chapter, someone who is appointed to the social services board despite having previously been removed from any public office by impeachment, or someone who is appointed to the social services board despite having been found guilty of corruption or malpractice in any public office.

While there are no explicit statutory procedures or grounds for removal of a social services board member, principles derived from North Carolina case law and statutes applicable to other types of appointed boards suggest that removal by an appointing authority is permitted under certain circumstances.

First, the removal of a social services board member is a quasi-judicial action. Certain due-process procedures must accompany any quasi-judicial proceeding.[42] If one looks to the statutes regarding consolidated human services boards and county boards of health as instructive, then due process would at least require providing the board member with (1) notice of the appointing authority's reason(s) for removal and (2) an opportunity to respond before the appointing authority takes final action to remove the board member from office.[43]

Second, the removal of a social services board member should be for *good cause.* Good cause for removing a social services board member generally means a significant failure to perform the member's duties or other conduct that makes the member's service on the board contrary to the public interest. Good cause would also include grounds that disqualify any individual from holding public office in North Carolina, such as willful failure to discharge official duties or constitutionally prohibited office holding.

What else might constitute good cause for removal? If one looks to the statutes regarding consolidated human services boards and county boards of health as instructive, then good cause for removing a social services board member would likely include

- commission of a felony or other crime involving moral turpitude;
- violation of a state law governing conflicts of interest;
- violation of a written policy adopted by the BOCC;
- habitual failure to attend meetings;
- conduct that tends to bring the office into disrepute; and
- failure to maintain qualifications for appointment.[44]

However, since North Carolina law does not establish grounds for removal of a social services board member, it is possible that an appointing authority might remove a social services board member on other grounds as well. Each county board of social services should adopt rules of procedure that establish procedures and grounds for removal of the third or fifth board member (the member appointed by the majority of the other board members).

Judicial Review of a Removal Decision

The removal of a social services board member by an appointing authority is a quasi-judicial action that, on the petition of the removed board member, may be reviewed by a superior court judge.[45] A social services board member who has been removed from office also may bring a declaratory judgment action in superior court regarding the removal decision.[46]

Notes

1. Chapter 108A, Section 3 of the North Carolina General Statutes (hereinafter G.S.).
2. G.S. 108A-3(b).
3. G.S. 108A, § 3(a)–(b).
4. G.S. 108A-5.
5. *See* N.C. Const. art. VI, § 10; G.S. 128-7; *see also* Baxter v. Danny Nicholson, Inc., 363 N.C. 829, 830 (2010) (holding that the authority of an appointed officer continues until the date on which his successor takes the oath of the office in question and thereby becomes qualified to begin performing the duties of that office).
6. *See* State *ex rel.* Pitts v. Williams, 260 N.C. 168 (1963); G.S. 108A-4; *see also* John L. Saxon, *Stay or Go? County Commissioners on Social Services Boards*, Popular Gov't, Winter 2000, at 27, 30–31.
7. G.S. 108A-4. State law does not impose a waiting period for the reappointment of a former social services board member following completion of two consecutive three-year terms. However, appointing authorities should not attempt to evade the purpose of the statutory term limits by appointing a person to succeed an incumbent board member with the understanding that the newly appointed board member will resign shortly thereafter, and the former board member will be reappointed to fill the remainder of the appointee's unexpired term.
8. G.S. 108A-4.
9. G.S. 108A-6.
10. *Id.*
11. *Id.*
12. *Id.*
13. G.S. 108A-3(c).
14. *See* Hall v. Wake Cty. Bd. of Elections, 280 N.C. 600, 605 (1972), *modified*, Lloyd v. Babb, 296 N.C. 416 (1979).
15. G.S. 153A-25.
16. A legal disqualification is any condition that, as a matter of constitutional, statutory, or common law, absolutely and unconditionally prohibits a person from being appointed to the county social services board or serving as a county social services board member.
17. N.C. Const. art. VI, § 9; G.S. 128-1.1. North Carolina's law limiting multiple office-holding is discussed in detail in A. Fleming Bell, II, Ethics, Conflicts, and Offices: A Guide for Local Officials (UNC School of Government, 2d ed. 2010).
18. G.S. 128-1.2.
19. N.C. Const. art. VI, § 8.
20. N.C. Const. art. VI, § 8. See also G.S. 13-1, regarding restoration of a felon's citizenship rights. For more information about restoration of citizenship rights, please see the UNC School of Government microsite *Relief from a Criminal Conviction*, available at https://www.sog.unc.edu/resources/microsites/relief-criminal-conviction/citizenship-rights.
21. G.S. 108A, §§ 47, 55(d).
22. Title 10A, Chapter 70E, Section .1105 of the North Carolina Administrative Code (hereinafter N.C.A.C.).
23. G.S. 143, §§ 318.9–.18. The state open meetings law is discussed in more detail in Frayda S. Bluestein & David M. Lawrence, Open Meetings and Local Governments in North Carolina: Some Questions and Answers (UNC School of Government, 8th ed. 2017). The open meetings law's requirements do not apply with respect to the

appointment of a county social services board member by a senior resident superior court judge.

24. G.S. 143-318.11(a)(6).
25. G.S. 143-318.13(b).
26. G.S. 143B-154; 10A N.C.A.C. 68, § .0302.
27. G.S. 153A-43.
28. *See* Frayda S. Bluestein, *Open Meetings and Other Legal Requirements for Local Government Boards*, *in* County and Municipal Government in North Carolina (Frayda S. Bluestein ed., UNC School of Government, 2d ed. 2014).
29. G.S. 108A-3. If a majority of the other social services board members are unable to agree, the appointment is made by the county's senior resident superior court judge. *Id.*
30. N.C. Const. art. VI, § 7; G.S. 11-7.1; G.S. 128-5; G.S. 153A-26. For more information about the language of the oath of office, please see Trey Allen, *One Oath or Two? What is the Oath of Office?*, Coates' Canons: NC Loc. Gov't L. (blog) (Jan. 27, 2017), https://canons .sog.unc.edu/2017/01/one-oath-or-two-what-is-the-oath-of-office/.
31. The authority of a "holdover" member continues until that member's successor takes and subscribes the oath of office. *See* Baxter v. Danny Nicholson, Inc., 363 N.C. 829 (2010).
32. G.S. 11-7.1.
33. G.S. 153A-26.
34. G.S. 14-229.
35. G.S. 128-5.
36. Frank v. Savage, 205 N.C. App. 183, 191 (2010) (finding that plaintiffs stated a cognizable claim that BOCC violated the law when revoking plaintiffs' appointments to the county board of social services).
37. *See* Kinsland v. Mackey, 217 N.C. 508 (1940) ("[T]he general rule is that in the absence of all constitutional or statutory provision for the removal of such public officers, the power of removal is incident to the power of appointment . . . .").
38. *See* G.S. 153A-77(c) (stating grounds for removal of consolidated human services board members); G.S. 130A-35 (stating grounds for removal of members of county board of health).
39. G.S. 128-5.
40. G.S. 14-230.
41. G.S. 128-2.
42. Berger v. New Hanover Cnty. Bd. of Comm'rs, No. 13 CVS 1942, 2013 WL 4792508, at *11 (N.C. Super. Sept. 5, 2013).
43. *See* G.S. 153A-77(c); G.S. 130A-35(g). These statutes are not applicable to or binding on the various appointing authorities with respect to removal of county social services board members, but they do provide an instructive analog in the absence of a social services statute regarding removal, given that these statutes relate to similarly situated governing boards for county agencies.
44. G.S. 153A-77(c); G.S. 130A-35(g).
45. G.S. 1-269; Russ v. Bd. of Educ. of Brunswick Cnty., 232 N.C. 128 (1950). This review may occur through a writ of recordari or certiorari.
46. G.S. 1, §§ 253–67 (declaratory judgment actions); Frank v. Savage, 205 N.C. App. 183, 191 (2010) (holding that appointees to county board of social services stated claim for declaratory relief that county board of commissioners acted outside its statutory authority in invalidating their appointments). A social services board member who has been removed from office also may seek judicial review of the removal through a *quo warranto* proceeding (an action brought to determine the right of a board member's successor to hold office). *See* G.S. 1, §§ 515–32 (quo warranto actions); State *ex rel.* Pitts v. Williams, 260 N.C. 168 (1963) (quo warranto action for order declaring individual to be the duly appointed and qualified member of a county welfare board).

Chapter 6

An Overview of the Powers and Duties of the County Board of Social Services

This chapter will provide a broad overview of the powers and duties that are assigned to the county board of social services by state law. Chapters 7, 8, 9, and 10 of this book take a closer look at how the board carries out some of these powers and duties.

The powers and duties of a consolidated human services board, which include some (but not all) of the responsibilities described in this chapter, are discussed in Chapter 16.

If a board of county commissioners (BOCC) dissolves a county social services board and assumes direct control of its activities, then the BOCC assumes all of the powers and responsibilities assigned to the county social services board by state law, including those described in this chapter.[1]

Sources of the Board's Legal Authority

A county social services board's authority, powers, and duties are based on state law. This means that the North Carolina General Assembly may enact legislation to change the powers or duties of social services boards. Many of the powers and duties of county social services boards are specified in Chapter 108A of the North Carolina General Statutes (hereinafter G.S.), while some are found in the North Carolina Administrative Code. State law also expressly provides that the state Social Services Commission, NCDHHS, or a BOCC may assign additional duties and responsibilities to county social services boards.[2]

County social services boards are prohibited from exercising powers that are not explicitly or implicitly granted to them by state law or that are vested by state law in another public official, board, or agency. For example, a county social services board cannot legally carry out the responsibilities of a county DSS director, even if the director's position is vacant.

When exercising their powers and duties, county social services boards are required to comply with applicable federal and state laws (for example, the requirements of the state open meetings law, the state public records law, the State Human Resources Act, and federal and state statutes prohibiting discrimination in employment).

The Board's Powers and Duties

State law authorizes the county social services board to carry out duties and responsibilities in the following areas.

The Director of Social Services

- The board appoints the county DSS director in accordance with the State Human Resources Act and the rules established by the State Human Resources Commission.[3]
- It determines, with the approval of the BOCC, the county DSS director's salary.[4]
- It consults with and advises the county DSS director about problems involving the county DSS.[5]
- It may evaluate the county DSS director's performance.[6]
- It may discipline or dismiss the county DSS director in accordance with the State Human Resources Act and the rules established by the State Human Resources Commission.[7]

Chapters 7 and 8 provide more detailed information on the board's responsibilities with respect to the county DSS director.

The Social Services Budget

The board assists the county DSS director in planning the proposed budget for the county DSS.[8] The board also has authority to transmit or present the proposed social services budget to the BOCC.[9] Chapter 10 provides more detailed information on the board's role in the budgeting process for the county department of social services.

The Board and Other Public Officials

The board is required to

- meet at least once per month, or more often if a special or emergency meeting is called by the board chair;[10]
- elect the board's chair;[11] and
- advise county and municipal authorities with respect to developing policies and plans to improve the community's social conditions.[12]

The board may also adopt rules of procedure for board meetings, for election of the board chair, and for removal of the third or fifth board member (the member appointed by the majority of the other members).

Chapter 13 provides more detailed information on board meetings and procedures.

Social Services Programs and Policies

Social services boards in North Carolina have relatively limited authority regarding social services policy and the administration of social services programs. However, state law does give county social services boards some responsibility to

- make certain decisions regarding public assistance programs,
- review cases of suspected fraud related to some public assistance programs,
- review some social services records, and
- enter into certain types of contracts.

Chapter 9 provides more detailed information on the board's powers and duties with respect to social services programs and policies.

Social Services Attorneys

Appointed county social services boards generally have no authority to appoint, retain, or hire an attorney to provide legal services to the county DSS. Two potential exceptions to this general rule are described below.

Contract Attorney

The BOCC must approve legal services contracts,[13] However, the BOCC may delegate this authority to the county manager, the county attorney, the county DSS director, or another county official or board (including the social services board).

Special County Attorneys for Social Services

State law allows the BOCC, with the approval of the county social services board, to appoint an attorney to serve as the "special county attorney for social services" or to designate the county attorney as the special county attorney for social services.[14] The duties of a special county attorney for social services may include providing legal advice to the county social services director, the county social services board, and the BOCC with respect to social services matters; representing the county board of social services in appeal proceedings and in any litigation relating to appeals; and performing any other duties that may be assigned by the county social services director, the county social services board, the BOCC, or state law.[15] A special county attorney for social services may be retained by the county on a contractual basis or hired as a county employee (though not as an employee of the county social services department). The compensation for a special county attorney for social services is determined by the BOCC.[16]

In practice, very few attorneys who provide legal services to county social services departments serve as special county attorneys for social services. Instead, counties typically use

- a "county attorney" model, under which the county DSS is represented by the county attorney or an assistant county attorney;
- a "staff attorney" model, under which DSS attorneys are hired by the county DSS director, are employees of the county DSS, and work under the director's supervision; or
- a "contract attorney" model, under which a private attorney is retained to represent the county DSS on a contractual or fee-for-service basis.

The various models for legal services used by county social services agencies are discussed in more detail in John L. Saxon's *Social Services in North Carolina*.[17]

Chapter 15 of this book discusses legal representation of social services board members who are sued in connection with their service on the board.

Limitations on the Board's Authority

County social services boards have no legal authority to make decisions regarding employees of the county DSS (other than the county DSS director) because state law vests that authority in the county DSS director.[18] This means that appointed county social services boards do not have the legal authority to

- hire, supervise, promote, discipline, or fire employees of the county social services department (other than the director);
- establish personnel policies for county social services employees;
- determine the salary schedule and employment benefits for county social services employees;
- approve or administer the county social services department's budget; or
- execute contracts involving social services employees.

A board of county commissioners that has assumed the powers and duties of a county board of social services, on the other hand, does have authority over some of these matters. For example, a BOCC has authority to

- enact personnel ordinances regarding annual leave, sick leave, hours of work, holidays, and the administration of the pay plan for county employees, which will apply to county social services employees if those county rules and regulations are filed with the director of the Office of State Human Resources;[19]
- adjust the salary ranges for the county DSS director and social services employees (subject to approval by the State Human Resources Commission);[20]
- approve the county social services department's budget;[21] and
- enter into contracts for the provision of social services.[22]

Even though appointed county social services boards do not have authority over DSS employment matters, they should be concerned with the compensation, working conditions, training, qualifications, and morale of county DSS employees. The compensation, training, and morale of county DSS employees all have a direct impact on the quality of the programs and services that the county DSS provides to the community. The social services board can encourage and support the DSS director to ensure that the county DSS has sufficient staff to perform its work and that county DSS staff receive adequate training to do their work. The compensation and working conditions of county DSS employees can make a significant difference in whether a county DSS can hire and retain qualified and talented staff.

Notes

1. Chapter 153A, Section 77(a) of the North Carolina General Statutes (hereinafter G.S.).
2. G.S. 108A-9(5). When the Social Services Commission or NCDHHS assigns additional duties and responsibilities to county social services boards, these additional duties and responsibilities may be specified in administrative rules (codified in the North Carolina Administrative Code) or other statements of policy or procedure. When a BOCC assigns additional duties or responsibilities to the county social services board, these additional duties or responsibilities should be specified in a resolution or ordinance adopted by the BOCC.
3. G.S. 108A, §§ 9(1), 12(a).
4. G.S. 108A-13.
5. G.S. 108A-9(3).
6. While this power is not explicitly granted to the board of social services in state law, it is implied in the board's authority to appoint and to dismiss the director.
7. G.S. 108A-12(a).
8. G.S. 108A-9(3).
9. G.S. 108A-9(4).
10. G.S. 108A-7. Consolidated human services boards, by contrast, are only required to meet at least quarterly. *See* G.S. 153A-77(c).
11. G.S. 108A-7.
12. G.S. 108A-9(2).
13. *See generally* G.S. 153A-12.
14. G.S. 108A-16.
15. G.S. 108A-18.
16. G.S. 108A-17.
17. John L. Saxon, Social Services in North Carolina (UNC School of Government, 2008).
18. *See* G.S. 108A-14(a)(2) (granting the DSS director sole authority to appoint county DSS personnel).
19. G.S. 126-9(a); G.S. 153A-94.
20. G.S. 126-9(b); *see also* Title 25, Chapter 01I of the North Carolina Administrative Code, Sections .2101–.2102, .2106–.2107.
21. G.S.159-13.
22. G.S. 153A-259.

Chapter 7

Recruiting, Selecting, and Appointing the County DSS Director

In a county with a standalone (nonconsolidated) department of social services, the county social services board has the exclusive authority to appoint, evaluate, discipline, and dismiss the county director of social services.[1] These responsibilities with respect to the director are among the board's most important powers, as they have the greatest potential to shape the overall trajectory of the county DSS. When exercising this authority, the board must comply with (1) the requirements set forth in the State Human Resources Act (SHRA) and rules adopted by the State Human Resources Commission (SHRC), (2) federal antidiscrimination laws, and (3) the procedures mandated by the state open meetings law.[2]

By contrast, a consolidated human services board does not have authority to appoint the consolidated human services director, though the board must advise the county manager on the decision and consent to the appointment.[3] Consolidated human services directors are discussed in Chapter 16 of this book.

This chapter will focus on the recruitment, selection, and appointment of the director of a county DSS.

The DSS Director's Role

When recruiting and selecting a candidate to serve as the DSS director, the board should understand the complex, challenging nature of the director's role. A day in the life of a county DSS director often involves making a multitude of tough decisions. For example, the director may have to make choices about end-of-life care for an elderly ward under guardianship, including emotionally challenging decisions like whether to remove life support. The director will have to make difficult judgment calls involving the safety and well-being of children, such as how to safely care for a child in DSS custody when no suitable placement is available for the child. The director will also likely be faced with challenging personnel issues, such as whether to terminate an employee with poor work performance when the department is short-staffed.

By law, every county DSS director is responsible for

- hiring and supervising employees of the county DSS;[4]
- administering the social services and public assistance programs established by Chapter 108A of the North Carolina General Statutes (hereinafter G.S.);[5]
- assessing reports of child abuse and neglect and taking appropriate action to protect children who are alleged to be abused, neglected, or dependent pursuant to North Carolina's Juvenile Code;[6]
- accepting children for placement in foster homes and supervising foster care placements;[7]
- investigating proposed adoptive placements and supervising adoptive placements;[8]
- filing legal proceedings seeking termination of parental rights with respect to certain juveniles placed in the custody of the DSS;[9]
- receiving and evaluating reports of abuse, neglect, or exploitation of disabled adults and taking appropriate action to protect disabled adults from abuse, neglect, or exploitation;[10]
- receiving and evaluating reports of financial exploitation of disabled and older adults and taking appropriate action to protect those adults from financial exploitation;[11]
- supervising the operation of adult care homes, including investigating complaints regarding the treatment of residents;[12]
- conducting and making decisions in local hearings in appeals by persons who have applied for or are receiving public assistance or social services;[13]
- serving as the guardian for adults found to be incompetent when appointed to do so by the clerk of superior court;[14]
- serving on the local Community Child Protection Team and reporting to the social services board regarding its activities;[15]
- serving on the county's Juvenile Crime Prevention Council;[16]
- arranging for the disposition of unclaimed bodies of deceased persons;[17]
- issuing certificates that authorize the employment of young people under age eighteen in accordance with applicable federal and state child-labor laws;[18]
- acting as the agent of the state Social Services Commission and NCDHHS with respect to work required by the Social Services Commission and NCDHHS in the county;[19]
- serving as the executive officer of the board of social services and acting as its secretary;[20] and
- performing other powers and duties specified by state law.

With respect to many of these powers and duties, the director may delegate to one or more staff of the county social services department the authority to act as the director's representative.[21] Ultimately, however, the county social services director remains responsible and accountable for the administration of the department and the actions of the department's staff. Accordingly, it is crucial for the board to choose a competent, knowledgeable, well-qualified candidate to serve as the director of the department.

Handling a Director Vacancy

If the director's position is vacant and the board is unable to appoint a new director immediately, the board should appoint an acting or interim social services director to serve until it appoints a new director.[22] An acting or interim social services director has the same powers and duties as a permanent social services director.[23] In the event of a sudden or unexpected director vacancy, the board must act quickly to appoint an individual to serve in this position so that the department has someone with legal authority to carry out and delegate the director's statutory responsibilities. In order to act swiftly, the board chair may need to call a special or emergency board meeting, as described in Chapter 13.

An emergency appointment as acting social services director—which may be made when an emergency situation requires the services of an employee before it is possible to identify a qualified applicant through the regular selection process—generally may not exceed sixty work days.[24] A temporary appointment as acting or interim social services director generally may not exceed twelve months.[25] If the director's position is vacant temporarily due to the incumbent director's leave of absence, it may be appropriate for the board to use a "time-limited appointment" if the acting director's services will be needed for a period of one year or less.[26] The board may want to consult with the county's human resources department and the local government program manager at the Office of State Human Resources (OSHR) to determine what type of appointment would be appropriate for an acting or interim director.

An incumbent member of the county board of social services may not serve as the acting or interim DSS director,[27] nor can the county board of social services collectively manage or operate the county DSS until an acting or interim director can be appointed.

Developing the Hiring Process

Deciding who should be appointed as the county's director of social services is one of the most significant decisions that a social services board may have to make. A county social services board needs to thoughtfully develop a legally compliant hiring process that ensures the board will select the best-qualified person to serve as the director. State rules require that the board's procedures for recruiting and selecting a new DSS director be validly related to the duties and responsibilities of the director's position and applied consistently to all applicants.[28]

The board's hiring strategy should outline the tasks that must be completed to recruit and appoint a new DSS director, identify who will be responsible for each task, and establish a timetable for the completion of each task.

Among other things, the board's strategy should ideally address

- how the position will be advertised,
- who will screen applications for the position,
- how candidates will be interviewed,
- how references will be checked,
- how the board will select its final candidate, and
- the minimum and maximum salary that can be offered.[29]

The steps in the hiring process are described in more detail below.

Legal Compliance

Though the county's human resources department does not have authority over personnel decisions regarding the DSS director, the county social services board should consult with the county's human resources department when designing the hiring process to ensure that the board's process is compliant with state and federal law. Likewise, the board should consider consulting with the local government program manager at OSHR regarding each step of the hiring process to ensure compliance with SHRC rules. Careful planning and advance consultation will help reduce the likelihood of litigation related to the board's recruitment process and hiring decisions.

Before starting the hiring process, the board should consult with the county's human resources department and the local government program manager at OSHR to determine whether any aspects of the county's personnel management system have been designated by the SHRC as "substantially equivalent" to the SHRA.[30] Counties that qualify for the substantially equivalent exemption in a particular category (e.g., "Classification/Compensation") may substitute their own county policies and procedures in place of the SHRA and its implementing regulations with respect to that category.[31] If the county's personnel management system has been approved as substantially equivalent in the areas of "Recruitment, Selection, and Advancement" or "Classification/Compensation," the board should comply with the county's policies and procedures in those areas, which could differ in some cases from the SHRA/SHRC requirements and procedures described in this chapter.

The rest of this chapter discusses hiring requirements and procedures established by the SHRA and the SHRC rules.

Position Description and Qualifications

State regulations require any candidate selected as the county DSS director to possess at least the minimum qualifications set forth in OSHR's *class specification* for a county director of social services.[32] Class specifications for positions in local government are available on OSHR's website.[33] All qualifications described in this section are from the class specification for the county social services director.

A person who is appointed as a county DSS director must have a master's degree in social work and two years of supervisory experience in the delivery of client services.[34] If the individual does not have a master's degree in social work, then the individual must have

- a bachelor's degree in social work and three years of supervisory experience in the delivery of client services, including at least one year in social services;
- a four-year degree and three years of supervisory experience in the delivery of client services, including two years in social services; or
- an equivalent combination of training and experience.

In addition to the aforementioned education and supervisory experience requirements, a person appointed as the DSS director is also required to have

- thorough knowledge of
  » the legal and philosophical basis for public welfare programs,
  » the principles and practice of social work, and
  » the principles and practices of management;
- knowledge of
  » the agency's organization and operation,
  » the agency's objectives, and
  » applicable federal and state laws, rules, and regulations; and
- the ability to
  » exercise sound judgment in analyzing situations and making decisions,
  » direct employees and programs in the various areas of responsibility, and
  » develop and maintain effective working relationships with the general public and with federal, state, and local officials.

In some cases, the board may feel that there are certain experiences or skills that would be needed to succeed in the DSS director position in a particular county that are not reflected in the OSHR class specification. For example, a board may want to require more years of supervisory experience than are required by the OHSR class specification. A county social services board may develop and include additional qualifications regarding training, experience, competencies, knowledge, skills, or abilities required for the DSS director's position only if (1) there is a documented business need for the additional qualifications, and (2) the additional qualifications bear a relationship to the minimum requirements in the class specification and the specific position description.[35]

The board should be careful not to add any qualifications that it would be prohibited from considering under state or federal law, such as qualifications related to sex, gender identity, sexual orientation, pregnancy, age, race, color, national origin, religion, or disability status.[36] State rules make clear that the board will bear responsibility for any "adverse effects" resulting from the use of selection standards that have not been established or approved by OSHR.[37]

Recruiting and Screening Applicants

After determining the minimum qualifications for the position, the social services board should put together a job vacancy notice that announces information about the position and the application process. The job vacancy notice must allow for an application period of at least seven days and must include the job title, salary range, duties, knowledge and skill requirements, minimum training and experience standards, closing date, and contact person for the application process.[38]

If the board decides to fill the director's position through recruitment within the county social services department, state rules require the board to post a job vacancy announcement for the position in a prominent location at the county social services department.[39] If the board decides to fill the director's position through open recruitment (by considering applicants outside of the county social services department), the board may want to consider additional avenues to attract external applicants, such as listing the position with the local NCWorks Career Center of the Division of Employment Security[40] and posting the position to online recruitment platforms. A county's human resources department may be able to assist the board in finding places to post the position.

Applications for the director's position should be submitted to the board or its designee and screened by the board, a subcommittee of the board, or the board's designee to ensure that they are complete and meet the minimum requirements established by the board and state rules. It is a best practice not to give a single individual the sole responsibility for screening applicants. If it is unclear whether a candidate meets the minimum qualifications for the position, the board may request that OSHR make the final determination as to whether the applicant meets the minimum qualifications.[41]

Though not legally required, it has been a long-standing practice for social services boards to send all applications for the DSS director position to the local government program manager at OSHR once the job posting has closed so that OSHR may determine whether all of the applicants meet the minimum qualifications. This practice helps to ensure that the social services board will only be interviewing applicants who meet the minimum requirements for the position and maximizes time spent on qualified applicants.

Out of those applicants who meet the minimum qualifications (as determined by the initial screening), the board or a subcommittee of the board must select a pool of the "most qualified" candidates, meaning those who are "substantially more qualified" for the role than other candidates.[42] The board must then select the new DSS director from this pool of most qualified applicants.[43] State rules do not specify the size of the "most qualified" pool, but selecting a relatively small pool may be advisable, since the board is required to notify all unsuccessful candidates within this pool after the board eventually selects the new director.[44] On the other hand, the board should also be careful to choose a "most qualified" pool that includes a sufficient number of viable candidates for the position, since the DSS director must ultimately be selected from this pool.

Any application screening or review that is conducted by the board or a subcommittee of the board must be done in a closed session, following a motion duly made and adopted at an open meeting.[45] More information about North Carolina's open meetings law, including requirements for closed sessions, is provided in Chapter 13.

Interviewing Candidates

From the pool of "most qualified" applicants, the board should determine which candidates it wishes to interview and schedule an interview with each such candidate.[46] When the board interviews a candidate or discusses the qualifications or suitability of candidates, it must do so at an official board meeting in accordance with the requirements of the state open meetings law, including providing notice of the meeting to the public.[47] Each interview and any discussion of a candidate's qualifications or suitability for the position should be conducted in a closed session of the meeting.[48] Ideally, all board members should participate in interviewing every candidate so they can all hear each candidate's responses and assess each candidate firsthand.

The board's interview process needs to be structured in such a way that it will allow members to make fair, consistent judgments about the candidates' qualifications, skills, and characteristics.[49] Questions asked of candidates should focus on the candidates' qualifications for the position, their professional experience, their motivation and desire to serve as the county's social services director, and how they might respond to the issues and challenges they may confront as the new director.[50] A structured interview process—ideally one developed with the assistance of a human resources professional   allows the board to treat each candidate fairly by asking each one the same questions. As a best practice, boards should consider developing and using a rating instrument that allows board members to evaluate each area of a candidate's knowledge, experience, and skills using a uniform scale.[51]

Board members should keep in mind that some interview questions are prohibited by federal and state antidiscrimination laws. The board should not ask candidates any questions regarding their race, religion, color, national origin, religious affiliation or beliefs, marital status, sex, sexual orientation, gender identity, pregnancy, children, age, or disability.[52]

Selection of a Final Candidate

After the interview process, the board must select a final candidate from the pool of applicants that it has determined are "most qualified" for the position.[53] As with every step in the hiring process, the board's method for selecting the new social services director from the final pool of candidates must be validly related to the duties and responsibilities of the vacancy to be filled.[54] The board must also give preference to applicants who served honorably in the armed services during designated periods of war (as defined in G.S. 108A-15(b)), to applicants who are veterans of the armed forces and who suffered disabling service-related injuries during peacetime, and to spouses, surviving spouses, and dependents of certain military veterans.[55]

Background and Reference Check

Prior to making an offer to the final candidate, the board should check the candidate's references and educational qualifications. The board should also run a background check that includes criminal convictions prior to appointing a candidate to the director position.[56]

IRS Publication 1075 and NCDHHS policy require local agencies to conduct background investigations on an applicant or employee who will have access to federal tax information in connection with their job duties.[57] This includes FBI fingerprinting; a check of local law enforcement agencies where the individual has lived, worked, or attended school within the last five years; and validation of the individual's eligibility to legally work in the United States.

The board should seek the assistance of the county's human resources professionals before engaging in any background check process, as there are a number of legal requirements involved in how the process is conducted and how the information gathered by the background check is used in a hiring decision.[58]

Final Appointment of the Director

Although the county social services board may discuss the qualifications of applicants during closed session, the board's decision to appoint an individual as the county social services director must be made by majority vote of a quorum of the board members present at an *open* session of an official board meeting.[59] The board's appointment of a county social services director is not subject to the approval of NCDHHS, the county human resources department, or any other public agency or official.[60] However, a county social services board may find it helpful to seek input and expertise from county human resources experts, NCDHHS, and the local government program manager at OSHR during the hiring process.

Following the selection of the DSS director, the board must provide written notice of non-selection to all unsuccessful candidates in the "most qualified" pool.[61] As a best practice, this notice of non-selection should be brief and should not elaborate on the reasons why a particular candidate was not chosen for the position.

When an individual is appointed as a new county social services director, that individual must serve a probationary appointment of three to nine months.[62] The length of the probationary period is dependent upon the complexity of the position and the rapidity of progress made by the individual in the position.[63] During the probationary period, the director may be dismissed for causes related to performance of duties or for personal conduct detrimental to the DSS without an automatic right of appeal or hearing. In such a scenario, the director must still be given notice of dismissal, including reasons for the dismissal.[64]

Determining the Director's Salary

State law provides that the salary of the county social services director is determined by the county social services board but must be approved by the board of county commissioners.[65] The director's salary must fall within the county's salary plan and schedule for county social services employees, which must be approved by the SHRC.[66]

Confidentiality of Applicant Information

Board members and any others involved in interviewing candidates or assessing the qualifications and suitability of candidates are required to protect the confidentiality of information regarding applicants for the director's position.[67] This means board members are prohibited from disclosing information about candidates gathered through the application process, the interview process, or the background check process. More information about the confidentiality of personnel information (which includes information about job applicants) is available in Chapter 8 of this book.

Notes

1. Chapter 108A, Sections 9(1) and 12 of the North Carolina General Statutes (hereinafter G.S.). A county social services board may not appoint a new county social services director unless the incumbent director has died or resigned, is retiring, or has been dismissed.
2. *See* G.S. 126, §§ 3, 4, 5(a)(2); Title 25, Subchapter I of the North Carolina Administrative Code (hereinafter N.C.A.C.).
3. G.S. 153A-77(e).
4. G.S. 108A-14(a)(2).
5. G.S. 108A-14(a)(3). These programs include, but are not limited to, Work First, Medicaid, Food and Nutrition Services, State-County Special Assistance, Low-Income Energy Assistance, and Foster Care and Adoption Assistance.
6. G.S. 108A-14(a)(11); *see also* G.S. 7B, §§ 300, 302, 307, 320, 500.
7. G.S. 108A-14(a)(12); *see also* G.S. 7B, §§ 505, 903, 904, 905, 910, 1905.
8. G.S. 108A, § 14(a)(6), (13); *see also* G.S. 48, §§ 1-109, 2-501, 3-201, 3-203, 3-303, 3-309, 3-601.
9. G.S. 7B-1103.
10. G.S. 108A-14(a)(14); *see also* G.S. 108A, §§ 103–06, 108, 109.
11. G.S. 108A-14(a)(15); *see also* G.S. 108A, §§ 115–17.
12. G.S. 108A-14(a)(8); *see also* G.S., §§ 2.11(b), 26.
13. G.S. 108A-79(f).
14. G.S. 35A, §§ 1202(4), 1213(d).
15. G.S. 7B, §§ 1407(b)(1), 1409.
16. G.S. 143B-846.
17. G.S. 130A-415.
18. G.S. 108A-14(a)(7); G.S. 95-25.5; 13 N.C.A.C. 12, § .0402.
19. G.S. 108A-14(a)(5).
20. G.S. 108A-14(a)(1).
21. G.S. 108A-14(b).
22. *See* 25 N.C.A.C. 01I, § .2002(g), (e).
23. *See In re* Appeal of Brunswick Cnty., 81 N.C. App. 391, 397 (1986).
24. 25 N.C.A.C. 01I, § .2002(g). When it is determined that an emergency appointment is necessary, all other requirements for appointments will be waived. No one individual may receive successive emergency appointments with the same department. At least three calendar months must elapse after the conclusion of the emergency appointment before that department can give the same individual another emergency appointment.
25. 25 N.C.A.C. 01I, § .2002(e).
26. *Id.* at (d)(1).
27. This is due to the common law rule against one person simultaneously holding incompatible offices. For a comprehensive discussion of the common law doctrine of incompatible office-holding, including applicable case law, please see A. FLEMING BELL, II, ETHICS, CONFLICTS, AND OFFICES: A GUIDE FOR LOCAL OFFICIALS ch. 7 (UNC School of Government, 2d ed. 2010).
28. 25 N.C.A.C. 01I, § .1905(a).
29. *See* VAUGHN MAMLIN UPSHAW, JOHN A. RIBLE IV, & CARL W. STENBERG, GETTING THE RIGHT FIT: THE GOVERNING BOARD'S ROLE IN HIRING A MANAGER 13, 26–27 (UNC School of Government, 2011).
30. As of January 2023, thirteen counties (Caldwell, Catawba, Chatham, Cleveland, Davie, Durham, Gaston, Iredell, Lincoln, Orange, Randolph, Rowan, and Scotland) had one or

more areas of their personnel management systems designated as substantially equivalent to the SHRA. (Email from Dominick D'Erasmo, N.C. Off. of State Hum. Res., on file with the author).

31. *See* G.S. 126-11(a), (b), (d); 25 N.C.A.C. 01I, § .2407.

32. 25 N.C.A.C. 01I, § .1905(b).

33. The OSHR class specifications for the position of County Social Services Director are available at https://files.nc.gov/ncoshr/migrated_files/Guide/CompWebSite/Class%20 Specs/09929.pdf.

34. All qualifications described in this section are from the OSHR class specification for the County Social Services Director position (*supra* note 33).

35. 25 N.C.A.C. 01I, §§ .1802(b), .1905(b)(1).

36. For more information, see *Prohibited Employment Policies/Practices*, U.S. Equal Opportunity Emp. Comm'n, https://www.eeoc.gov/prohibited-employment-policiespractices (last visited Mar. 31, 2023).

37. 25 N.C.A.C. 01I, § .1802(b).

38. *Id.,* § .1902(b).

39. *Id.*

40. *Id.* at (c).

41. *Id.,* § .1905(b)(4).

42. *Id.,* § .1905(a)(1).

43. *Id.*

44. *Id.* at (a)(4).

45. G.S. 143, § 318.11(a)(6), (c).

46. 25 N.C.A.C. 01I, § .1905(a)(3).

47. *See generally* G.S. 143, art. 33C.

48. G.S. 143-318.11(a)(6).

49. 25 N.C.A.C. 01I, § .1905(a)(2) requires that selection procedures and methods (including interview processes) be validly related to the duties and responsibilities of the vacancy to be filled.

50. *See* 25 N.C.A.C. 01I, § .1905(a)(2). For more information on lawful and unlawful interview questions, see Diane M. Juffras, Recruitment and Selection Law for Local Government Employers ch. 5 (UNC School of Government, 2013).

51. *See* Vaughn Mamlin Upshaw, How Are We Doing? Evaluating Manager and Board Performance 12–13 (UNC School of Government, 2014).

52. *See* G.S. 126-16; see also, Juffras, *supra* note 50. Federal laws implicating these protected characteristics include Title VII of the Civil Rights Act of 1964, the Americans with Disabilities Act, and the Age Discrimination in Employment Act of 1967. For more information on federal requirements, see U.S. Equal Emp. Opportunity Comm'n, *supra* note 36.

53. 25 N.C.A.C. 01I, § .1905(a).

54. *Id.* at (a)(2).

55. *See* G.S. 128-15; G.S. 126-83; Davis v. Vance Cnty. Dep't of Soc. Servs., 91 N.C. App. 428 (1988); Wright v. Blue Ridge Mental Health Auth., 134 N.C. App. 668 (1999).

56. Though conducting a background check is not legally required unless the director will have access to federal tax information, it is a best practice in light of the nature of the DSS director's role. In addition to having responsibility over agency employees and a substantial budget, the DSS director's position involves access to vulnerable children and adults and to highly confidential information regarding DSS clients.

57. Internal Revenue Serv., IRS Pub. 1075, Tax Information Security Guidelines for Federal, State and Local Agencies: Safeguards for Protecting Federal Tax Returns and Return Information (rev. Nov. 2021), https://www.irs.gov/pub/irs-pdf/ p1075.pdf; *see also* N.C. Dep't of Health & Hum. Servs., Document CSS_19_39a1, Background Checks for Potential Employees, Employees, and Contractors

Access to Federal Tax Information, https://www.ncdhhs.gov/documents/files/dss/dcdl/childsupportservices/css-19-39a1/download. The NCDHHS policy applies specifically to applicants and employees who will have access to federal tax information in connection with child support enforcement duties.

58. For more information about the legal ramifications of the background check process, including the decision to use a candidate's criminal history as a factor in the hiring decision, please see JUFFRAS, *supra* note 50, ch. 8.

59. G.S. 143-318.11(a)(6).

60. G.S. 108A, §§ 9(1), 12. The board of county commissioners, however, must approve the amount of the director's salary. G.S. 108A-13.

61. 25 N.C.A.C. 01I, § .1905(a)(4).

62. *Id.*, § .2002(a).

63. *Id.* at (a)(4).

64. *Id.* at (a)(5). Though the state rules do not require the notice of dismissal to be in writing, it is a best practice to always provide written notice of a dismissal or other disciplinary action.

65. G.S. 108A-14.

66. G.S 126-9(b) authorizes boards of county commissioners to adjust the salary ranges for positions subject to the SHRA so that the ranges will conform to local financial ability and fiscal policy. These adjustments are subject to approval by the SHRC. *See also* 25 N.C.A.C. 01I, §§ .2101–.2102; .2106–.2107.

67. *See* G.S. 153A-98; Elkin Trib., Inc. v. Yadkin Cnty. Bd. of Cnty. Comm'rs, 331 N.C. 735 (1992).

Chapter 8

Advising, Evaluating, Disciplining, and Dismissing the Director of Social Services

In a county with a standalone (nonconsolidated) county department of social services, the county social services board has the exclusive authority to appoint the county DSS director. Based on that authority, the county social services board is responsible for providing general supervision of the director, including evaluating the director's performance and advising the director regarding issues that affect the county DSS. The county social services board also has the sole authority to discipline or dismiss the director. This chapter discusses each of these important responsibilities.

By contrast, a consolidated human services board does not have authority to appoint, discipline, or dismiss the director of a consolidated human services agency. The relationship between a consolidated human services agency and its director is discussed in Chapter 16 of this book.

Advising the Director

The county social services board has a statutory duty to consult with the director about problems relating to the director's office or the county DSS.[1] The board does not have legal authority to overrule or interfere with the director's management decisions, but it does have a responsibility to offer guidance and support regarding problems facing the director or the county DSS as a whole. A regular evaluation process, combined with an ongoing open dialogue with the director, can help the board identify, understand, and address problems affecting the department. Understanding and advising the director on emerging problems may help to improve service delivery, staff morale, and legal compliance within the county DSS.

If the board is dissatisfied with the director's decisions or management, the board should work with the director toward a resolution if possible, including working to understand the director's perspective, providing feedback on the director's performance, and taking disciplinary action if needed.

Evaluating the Director

Due to its express authority to appoint and dismiss the DSS director, the county board of social services has the implied authority and responsibility to evaluate the director's performance. State law, however, does not provide a procedure for evaluating the county social services director. This means that each county social services board may adopt its own policies and procedures for evaluating the director. Accordingly, each board may decide how frequently to evaluate the director, when the evaluation process will occur, what standards and criteria to use in the evaluation, and what process to use for conducting evaluations.

Regular evaluations of the director's performance are important for several reasons:

1. They provide important feedback to the director about whether the director is meeting the board's expectations. They allow the board to review the director in a *proactive* way, as opposed to merely *reacting* to a crisis or problem.
2. They help to detect and solve problems and concerns within the DSS before they escalate into more serious situations.
3. They give the director and the board an opportunity to clarify areas of misunderstanding about the director's role, the board's role, or issues happening within DSS.
4. They give the board an opportunity to better understand the external and internal challenges affecting the director's performance.
5. They allow the board to identify, acknowledge, and reward good performance.
6. They allow the board to document performance concerns and how those concerns are addressed over time. If the board ultimately has to discipline or dismiss a director for performance reasons, the board should have documentation of the concerns that led to the discipline or dismissal.

In some counties, the county manager or county human resources department may want all county employees to be evaluated using a similar evaluation tool or on a similar schedule. Since merit-based salary increases may be tied to the county's evaluation process, the board should learn what the county manager or county human resources department expects before developing an evaluation process for the DSS director.

When developing a procedure for evaluating the DSS director, social services boards may want to consider the following best practices derived from public administration literature:[2]

Time
The board needs to devote sufficient time to planning the evaluation process, conducting each evaluation, and discussing the evaluation results with the director.

Criteria

Prior to the beginning of the evaluation process, the board should agree on standardized evaluation criteria for the director so that the director's performance can be measured in a consistent way from one evaluation to the next. The board should work with the director to determine a set of criteria that is specifically tailored for the county at issue. This might include criteria related to leadership of employees, fiscal management, staff recruitment and retention, program management and service delivery, relationship-building with state and local officials, creative problem-solving, or other relevant categories.

Frequency

The board should decide how frequently to engage in the evaluation process. If a newly appointed director is serving a probationary period of employment, the board should evaluate the director before the end of that period to decide whether the director should be retained. After a director has completed the probationary period, the board should evaluate the director on an annual basis (or more frequently, if desired).

Form

The board should agree on an evaluation form to capture and measure the board's evaluation criteria and goals for the director's performance. The questions and categories on the form should be easy for board members to understand and should reflect the board's agreed-upon evaluation criteria. State law does not prescribe any particular evaluation form or template for DSS directors.

Process

The board should develop a process to collect and discuss feedback regarding the director's performance. A common process is to ask each board member to evaluate the director using the standards and methods specified by the board, meet to discuss the evaluations completed by each member, synthesize the individual evaluations into a single final evaluation, and discuss the final evaluation with the director.

Flexibility

The board should periodically discuss, revisit, and update its evaluation process to determine what is working well and what could be improved. For example, the board may discover that certain performance criteria are unrealistic or no longer applicable. The board may find that certain evaluation questions elicit more helpful information than others. The board should be flexible, curious, and open to continuous improvement in how it evaluates the director. This may include seeking input from the director or from boards of social services in other counties about current best practices for performance evaluations.

Director Input

As a best practice, the board should seek and consider the director's input in developing the evaluation process. What are the director's goals for professional development? What are the director's goals for the department? How does the director think progress toward those goals should be measured and evaluated? What would the director like to learn from each evaluation process? The board and the director can discuss these questions together when developing evaluation criteria and expectations.

Director Self-Assessment

The board may want to invite the director to complete a self-assessment as part of each evaluation process. A self-assessment allows the board to learn about the director's accomplishments, challenges, and perceptions of the director's own performance.

Open and Honest Dialogue

Ideally, the director should not be surprised by the results of an evaluation, regardless of whether that evaluation reflects poor performance or excellent performance. The board should address problems with the director as they arise, rather than waiting for a formal evaluation to express concerns or provide critiques. Likewise, when the director's work merits praise and encouragement, the board should provide that positive feedback in a timely fashion.

The board should strive to be honest with the director, both in its routine feedback and in any formal evaluation process. It can sometimes be difficult for board members to provide candid feedback, but doing so is crucial to the director's long-term success.

Evaluation Procedures

The board's discussion of the county DSS director's performance must take place at an official meeting of the board but may be conducted during a closed session called pursuant to Chapter 143, Section 318.11(a)(6) of the North Carolina General Statutes (hereinafter G.S.)

A board could take the following approach to the performance evaluation, based on best practices derived from public administration literature:[3]

1. Each board member is given an opportunity to express thoughts and conclusions regarding the director's performance with respect to each performance standard or criterion.
2. The DSS director is given an opportunity to provide a self-assessment to the board.

3. The board discusses any differences among members' evaluations and considers any information from other sources, like the director's self-assessment.
4. If possible, the board agrees on a single rating or written summary for each of the criteria or standards covered by the evaluation.
5. The board provides the director a copy of its final evaluation and discusses it with the director. During that discussion, the board should highlight any areas of the director's performance that are unsatisfactory or need improvement and emphasize areas that show growth or excellence.
6. The board and the director agree on any actions the board feels the director should take to improve the director's performance and discuss the board's expectations for the director's performance in the coming year. This may include asking the director to develop performance goals for the coming year.

All information related to the board's evaluation of the director is part of the director's personnel record and is protected by the confidentiality requirements applicable to county employee personnel files.[4] Those confidentiality requirements are discussed in more detail later in this chapter.

For a more detailed resource on developing and conducting performance evaluations, please read Vaughn Mamlin Upshaw's book, *How Are We Doing? Evaluating Manager and Board Performance.*[5] While this book is tailored toward evaluating city and county managers, it provides principles and recommendations that may also be useful in evaluating the director of a county department.

Disciplining or Dismissing the Director

The county social services board has the exclusive legal authority to discipline or dismiss (terminate) the county social services director.[6] When disciplining or dismissing the director, the board must comply with the requirements of the State Human Resources Act (SHRA) and the rules adopted by the State Human Resources Commission (SHRC). If a county social services board is considering disciplining or dismissing the director, the board should immediately request guidance from the county's human resources office or the Office of State Human Resources' local government team on how to comply with the requirements of the SHRA and the SHRC rules.

All discussions by the board regarding the director's performance, competence, fitness, or character—as well as any investigation or hearing concerning any complaint, charge, or grievance by or against the director—must take place at an official board meeting and during a closed session pursuant to G.S. 143-318.11(a)(6). However, if the board determines that the director should be dismissed, the *final* action to dismiss the director must be taken by the board in an open meeting and not during a closed session.[7]

How Attaining Career Status Affects Discipline and Dismissal

Depending on the nature of the director's appointment and length of service, the director may be a probationary employee, a non-career-status employee (for example, in a time-limited or temporary appointment), or an employee with *career status*. For more information on the various types of appointments, please see the *State Human Resources Manual*'s "Appointment Types and Career Status" policy, available on the Office of State Human Resources' website.[8]

Under the SHRA and the SHRC rules, a director receives greater protection from discipline and dismissal if the director is a career status employee. To attain career status, the director must be (1) in a permanent position with a permanent appointment and (2) continuously employed in a position subject to the SHRA for the immediate twelve preceding months.[9] Once the director attains career status under the SHRA, that individual must be given due process prior to termination.[10] Specifically, a director who has earned career status can be dismissed, suspended, or demoted for disciplinary reasons only for "just cause," as described below.[11]

At any time during the period *prior to* achieving career status, including during the probationary period, a director may be disciplined or dismissed for causes related to performance of duties or for personal conduct detrimental to the county DSS without any right of appeal or hearing.[12] The director must be given notice of dismissal, including reasons for the dismissal.[13] It is a best practice to put such a notice in writing.

Disciplining or Dismissing a Director with Career Status

A county social services director who has attained career status may be disciplined or dismissed by the county social services board only based on (1) unsatisfactory job performance or (2) unacceptable personal conduct.[14]

Unsatisfactory Job Performance

Unsatisfactory job performance is defined as "work-related performance that fails to meet job requirements as specified in the job description, work plan, or as directed by the management of the work unit or agency."[15] The SHRC rules provide that this category is intended to "assist and promote improved employee performance, rather than to punish" and that discipline under the category is "intended to bring about a permanent improvement in job performance."[16] For example, it may be appropriate to discipline the director (e.g., issuing a written warning) under this category when the board believes that the director's performance can be improved through additional feedback, dialogue, and accountability.

In order to be dismissed for a current incident of unsatisfactory job performance, the director must first receive at least *two* disciplinary actions.[17] First, the director must receive one or more written warnings (under the SHRC rules, a written warning is a disciplinary action).[18] Second, the director must receive an additional written warning or other disciplinary action that notifies the director that failure to make the required performance improvements may result in dismissal.

Unacceptable Personal Conduct

Unacceptable personal conduct is defined as

(1) conduct on or off the job that is related to the employee's [i.e., the director's] job duties and responsibilities for which no reasonable person should expect to receive prior warning;

(2) conduct that constitutes a violation of State or federal law;

(3) conviction of a felony that is detrimental to or impacts the employee's service to the agency;

(4) the willful violation of work rules;

(5) conduct unbecoming an employee that is detrimental to the agency's service;

(6) the abuse of client(s), patient(s), or a person(s) over whom the employee has charge or to whom the employee has a responsibility, or of an animal owned or in the custody of the agency;

(7) falsification of an employment application or other employment documentation;

(8) insubordination that is the willful failure or refusal to carry out an order from an authorized supervisor;

(9) absence from work after all authorized leave credits and benefits have been exhausted; or

(10) failure to maintain or obtain credentials or certifications.[19]

Even one act of unacceptable personal conduct that falls in one of these categories may constitute just cause for discipline, up to and including dismissal.[20]

Another category of unacceptable personal conduct is "grossly inefficient job performance." Grossly inefficient job performance means the director

fails to perform job requirements as specified in the job description, work plan, or as directed by the management of the work unit or agency and that failure results in:

(1) death or serious harm or the creation of the potential for death or serious harm, to a client(s), an employee(s), members of the public or to a person(s) over whom the [director] has responsibility; or

(2) the loss of or damage to agency property or funds that result in a serious impact on the agency or work unit.[21]

The director may be dismissed for a current incident of unacceptable personal conduct (including grossly inefficient job performance) without *any* prior active disciplinary actions.[22] The board may impose any level of discipline—including a suspension, demotion, or dismissal—without warning if it is based on unacceptable personal conduct.[23] Figure 8.1 illustrates the avenues of disciplinary action and dismissal available to county DSS boards.

Figure 8.1. Disciplining or Dismissing a County DSS Director

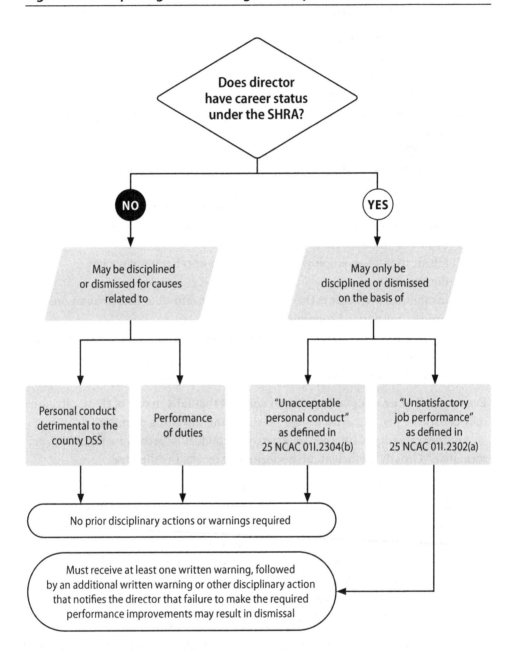

Forms of Discipline Other than Dismissal

Written Warning

The board may elect to issue a written warning for grossly inefficient job performance or unacceptable personal conduct. The written warning must inform the director

- that it is a written warning, and not some other nondisciplinary process (e.g., counseling);
- what specific issues form the basis for the warning;
- what specific corrections, if any, must be made to address these specific issues;
- the time frame allowed for making those corrections (grossly inefficient job performance and unacceptable personal conduct require immediate correction);
- the consequences of failing to make the required corrections; and
- what appeal rights, if any, are provided by agency policy.[24]

The director may appeal a written warning only if the county's personnel ordinance or grievance procedure allows employees to appeal disciplinary warnings.

Disciplinary Suspension Without Pay

The director may be suspended without pay for disciplinary purposes[25] (1) for unsatisfactory job performance after the receipt of at least one prior disciplinary action, or (2) without any prior warning for causes relating to any form of unacceptable personal conduct or grossly inefficient job performance.[26] Prior to placing the director on disciplinary suspension without pay, the board must conduct a pre-disciplinary conference with the director (described in more detail later in this chapter).[27] The board must also provide the director with a written statement setting forth the specific acts or omissions that are the reasons for the suspension and stating the director's appeal rights.[28]

Demotion

Demotion may be made on the basis of either unsatisfactory job performance or unacceptable personal conduct (including grossly inefficient job performance).[29] The director may be demoted for unsatisfactory job performance after receiving at least one prior disciplinary action.[30] The director may be demoted for unacceptable personal conduct (including grossly inefficient job performance) without any prior disciplinary action.[31] The director must receive written notice of the specific reasons for the demotion, as well as notice of any applicable appeal rights.[32] Prior to the decision to demote the director for disciplinary reasons, the board must conduct a pre-disciplinary conference with the director (described in more detail later in this chapter).[33]

A disciplinary demotion may be accomplished in one of three ways:

1. The director may be demoted to a different role in a lower pay grade with a reduction in salary rate.

2. The director may be demoted to a different role in a lower pay grade without a reduction in salary rate.

3. The director may remain in the same role (with the same pay grade), but with a reduction in salary rate.[34]

In any event, the resulting salary rate must fall within the salary range for the applicable pay grade (for either the director's role or the role to which the director is being demoted).[35] Since the board's decisions regarding the director's salary must be approved by the board of county commissioners, the board of county commissioners must also concur in any decisions to reduce the director's salary rate.[36]

Required Procedures Before Disciplining or Dismissing a Director Who Has Achieved Career Status

Pre-disciplinary Conference

Before taking action to dismiss a director, demote a director, or suspend the director without pay on the basis of unsatisfactory job performance or unacceptable personal conduct, the board must conduct a pre-disciplinary conference.[37] The purpose of the pre-disciplinary conference is to review the recommendation for discipline with the director, listen to and consider any information put forth by the director, and ensure that the disciplinary decision is sound and not based on misinformation or mistake.[38] The director must be given prior oral or written notice (as far in advance as is practical under the circumstances) of the time and location of the conference and the basis for the possible dismissal, suspension, or demotion.[39]

If the pre-disciplinary conference is being held in connection with a possible dismissal, the SHRC rules set forth some additional procedural requirements. No witnesses or attorneys (representing the director or the board) are permitted to attend the pre-dismissal conference.[40] Security personnel may be present when, in the discretion of the board, a need for security exists.[41] During the conference, the board must give the director notice of the recommendation for dismissal, including specific reasons for the proposed dismissal and a summary of the information supporting that recommendation.[42] Though the SHRC rules allow this notice to be oral, it is a best practice to provide the notice in writing. The director must have an opportunity to respond to the proposed dismissal action and to offer information or arguments in support of the director's position.[43] The board must make every effort to ensure that the director has a full opportunity during the conference to set forth any available information in opposition to the recommendation to dismiss.[44] However, this opportunity does not include the option to present witnesses.

After the Pre-disciplinary Conference

After the pre-disciplinary conference, the board must review and consider the director's response and then decide whether the director should be suspended, demoted, or dismissed. These discussions must take place at an official meeting of the board but may be conducted during a closed session called pursuant to G.S. 143-318.11(a)(6).

If the board decides to demote or suspend the director, it must provide the director with a written statement setting forth the specific acts or omissions that are the reasons for the suspension or demotion and advising the director of any applicable appeal rights.[45] In the case of a demotion, the board must also inform the director of how and to what extent the demotion will affect the director's salary rate or pay grade.[46]

If the board decides to dismiss the director, it must take the final action to do so during an open meeting.[47] The board must also deliver a written letter of dismissal to the director containing the specific reasons for dismissal, the effective date of the dismissal, and the director's appeal rights.[48] The letter of dismissal must be delivered to the director in person or sent by certified mail, return receipt requested, to the director's last known address.[49] This dismissal decision must not be communicated to the director prior to the beginning of the next business day following the conclusion of the pre-dismissal conference or after the end of the second business day following the conclusion of the pre-dismissal conference.[50] In other words, the board cannot hand the director a letter of dismissal immediately following the conclusion of the pre-dismissal conference.

If the dismissal is for unsatisfactory job performance, the board has the authority to determine the effective date of the dismissal.[51] The effective date of the dismissal must not be earlier than when the letter of dismissal is delivered, nor may it be more than fourteen calendar days after the notice of dismissal.[52] If the director has permanent status (as opposed to being in a probationary period) and is dismissed for unsatisfactory job performance, the board may (at its discretion) give the director up to two weeks' working notice.[53] Alternatively, the board may (at its discretion) choose to give the director up to two weeks' pay in lieu of working notice.[54] Importantly, the board's ability to give the director working notice or pay in lieu of notice is applicable only to dismissal for unsatisfactory job performance, *not* to dismissal for unacceptable personal conduct.[55]

The Director's Appeal Rights After Discipline or Dismissal

If the board takes action to discipline or dismiss a county DSS director with career status, the director has a right to appeal the decision. The steps in that appeal process are described in this section.

1. Local Appeal

A director with career status who has been demoted, suspended, or dismissed for unsatisfactory job performance or unacceptable personal conduct has the right to appeal the demotion, suspension, or dismissal.[56] The director has fifteen calendar days from the date when the director receives written notice of the demotion, suspension, or dismissal to file an appeal in accordance with any applicable county personnel ordinance or grievance policy (the "agency grievance procedure").[57] If the director does not appeal the board's action through the applicable agency griev-ance procedure within fifteen calendar days, then the director has no right to file a contested case with the Office of Administrative Hearings (OAH).[58] If the director appeals the board's action through the agency grievance procedure, then the decision made at the conclusion of the director's appeal through the grievance procedure constitutes the "final agency decision."[59]

2. Appeal to the Office of Administrative Hearings.

If the director has completed the local agency grievance process and is not satisfied with the final agency decision, or is unable to obtain a final agency decision within ninety days from the date the grievance was filed, the director may file a petition for a contested case hearing in OAH.[60] The director must file a petition for a contested case hearing within thirty calendar days after receiving the final agency decision and serve a copy of the petition on the board.[61] If the director files a petition with OAH, OAH will assign an administrative law judge (ALJ) to hear the case.[62] The director and board will be given at least fifteen days' notice of the hearing.[63]

At the hearing, both the board and the director have the right to be represented by legal counsel, to call, examine, and cross-examine witnesses, to present evidence, and to make legal arguments to the ALJ.[64] If the director alleges that the suspension, demotion, or dismissal occurred without just cause, *the board has the burden of proving*, by a preponderance of the evidence, that it was for just cause.[65] After the hearing, the ALJ is required to issue a final decision or order that contains findings of fact and conclusions of law.[66] OAH will send a copy of the ALJ's final decision to the board and director.[67]

3. Judicial Review by Superior Court

The director may seek judicial review of the ALJ's decision by filing a petition in superior court pursuant to Article 4 of the state Administrative Procedure Act.[68] A petition for judicial review must be filed within thirty days of service of the ALJ's final decision and served on all parties to the OAH proceeding.[69] The superior court judge may reverse or modify the ALJ's decision if the judge determines that the decision was unconstitutional, exceeded statutory authority, was made upon unlaw-ful procedure, was affected by other errors of law, was unsupported by substantial evidence, or was arbitrary, capricious, or an abuse of discretion.[70]

The director or the board may appeal the superior court decision to the North Carolina Court of Appeals.[71]

Investigating the Director

What if the board has serious concerns about allegations against the DSS director but does not yet have enough information to take disciplinary action? The board may place the director in "investigation status" with pay, which does not constitute a disciplinary action under the SHRA.[72] Investigation status is used to temporarily remove an employee from active work status. The board may only place the director in investigation status

1. to investigate allegations of performance or conduct deficiencies that would constitute just cause for disciplinary action;
2. to provide time within which to schedule and conduct a pre-disciplinary conference; or
3. to avoid disruption of the workplace or to protect the safety of persons or property.[73]

The board is prohibited from placing the director in investigation status for the purpose of delaying its decision on the director's work status pending the resolution of a civil or criminal court matter involving the director.[74]

The board must notify the director in writing of the reasons for investigatory placement no later than the second scheduled work day after the beginning of the placement.[75] An investigatory placement with pay may last no longer than thirty calendar days without written notice of extension by the board. When an extension beyond the thirty-day period is required, the board must advise the director in writing of the extension, the length of the extension, and the specific reasons for the extension. If no action has been taken by the board by the end of the thirty-day period and no further extension has been imposed, the board must either take appropriate disciplinary action on the basis of the findings upon investigation or return the director to active work status.

Confidentiality of Personnel Information Regarding the Director

State law requires county employee personnel information to be kept confidential.[76] This includes information about the DSS director's application, selection, performance, promotions, demotions, transfers, suspension, other disciplinary actions, evaluations, leave, compensation, and dismissal.[77]

However, the following information is a matter of public record about any county employee, including the DSS director:

- the employee's name;
- the employee's age;
- the date of the employee's original employment or appointment;
- the terms of any employment contract, whether written or oral;
- the employee's current position, title and salary;
- the date and amount of each increase or decrease in employee's salary (including pay, benefits, incentives, bonuses, and deferred and all other forms of compensation);
- the date and type of the employee's most recent promotion, demotion, transfer, suspension, separation, or other change in position classification;

- the date and general description of the reasons for each promotion;
- the date and type of each dismissal, suspension, or demotion for disciplinary reasons (if the disciplinary action was a dismissal, a copy of the written notice of the final decision setting forth the specific acts or omissions that are the basis of the dismissal is also a matter of public record); and
- the office or station to which the employee is currently assigned.[78]

As a general rule, county social services board members should not disclose any personnel information regarding the county DSS director except for the categories of information that are a matter of public record, as described above. However, there are a number of exceptions in the law that allow the disclosure of confidential county employee personnel information in certain circumstances. Board members can look to G.S. 153A-98 to learn more about these exceptions. Board members may also look to Chapter 7 of *Public Records Law for North Carolina Local Governments, Second Edition*, by David M. Lawrence, as a resource for understanding the exceptions.[79]

The Board's Authority Regarding Social Services Employees

As discussed earlier in Chapter 6, county social services boards have no legal authority to hire, evaluate, supervise, promote, discipline, or dismiss any county DSS employees other than the county DSS director. Accordingly, board members should refrain from any action that might impinge upon the director's authority to hire, supervise, or discipline social services employees. For example, it is generally inappropriate for board members to attempt to insert themselves into DSS personnel disputes, hiring processes, or disciplinary matters involving employees other than the director. Board members may express opinions about DSS personnel matters, but do not have authority to require or demand that the DSS director take particular actions with respect to individual social services employees (e.g., hiring, firing, or discipline).

Notes

1. Chapter 108A, Section 9(3) of the North Carolina General Statutes (hereinafter G.S.).
2. *See* Vaughn Mamlin Upshaw, How Are We Doing? Evaluating Manager and Board Performance (UNC School of Government, 2014); *see also* Margaret S. Carlson, *"How Are We Doing?" Evaluating the Performance of the Chief Administrator,* Popular Gov't, Winter 1994, at 24.
3. *See* Upshaw, *supra* note 2; Carlson, *supra* note 2.
4. G.S. 153A-98.
5. Upshaw, *supra* note 2.
6. G.S. 108A-12(a).
7. G.S. 143-318.11(a)(6).
8. N.C. Off. of State Hum. Res., *Appointment Types and Career Status Policy, in* State Human Resources Manual (updated Feb. 15, 2023), https://oshr.nc.gov/media/5248/open.
9. G.S. 126-1.1(a). Though this status applies to local government employees, the SHRA and OSHR policies refer to it as "career State employee" status. To avoid confusion, this book will use the term *career status.*
10. *See* Peace v. Emp. Sec. Comm'n, 349 N.C. 315, 322 (1998).
11. G.S. 126, §§ 1.1, 35(a); *see also* Title 25, Chapter 01I, Section .2301 of the North Carolina Administrative Code (hereinafter N.C.A.C.).
12. 25 N.C.A.C. 01I, § .2301(b).
13. *Id.*
14. *Id.*, § .2301(c)–(d).
15. *Id.*, § .2302(a).
16. 25 N.C.A.C. 01J, § .0605, as referenced in 25 N.C.A.C. 01I, § 2302(b) ("Agencies shall apply this Rule consistent with the requirements of 25 NCAC 01J .0605.").
17. 25 N.C.A.C. 01I, § .2302(c).
18. *See id.*, §§ .2301(a)(1), .2302(c).
19. *Id.*, § .2304(b).
20. Watlington v. Dep't of Soc. Servs. Rockingham Cnty., 261 N.C. App. 760, 768 (2018) (citing Hilliard v. N.C. Dep't of Corr., 173 N.C. App. 594, 597 (2005)).
21. 25 N.C.A.C. 01I, § .2303(a).
22. *Id.*, §§ .2304(a), .2303(b).
23. *Id.*, § .2304(a).
24. *Id.*, § .2305.
25. An investigatory leave *with* pay, which may be used to temporarily remove the director from work status in certain circumstances, does not constitute a disciplinary action. *Id.*, § .2309(c).
26. 25 N.C.A.C. 01I, § .2306(a).
27. *Id.*
28. *Id.*
29. *Id.*
30. *Id.*, § .2307(a)(1).
31. *Id.* at (a)(2)–(3).
32. *Id.* at (a)(1).
33. *Id.*, § .2307(c).
34. *Id.*, § .2307(b).
35. *Id.*, § .2307(b)(3).

36. *See* G.S. 108A-13.
37. 25 N.C.A.C. 01I, § .2308.
38. *Id.*, § .2308(4)(d).
39. *Id.*, § .2308.
40. *Id.*, § .2308(4)(d)–(e).
41. *Id.* at (4)(d).
42. *Id.* at (4)(e).
43. *Id.*
44. *Id.*
45. *Id.*, § .2308(2)(c)–(d), (3)(d), (3)(f). The notice of appeal rights must be in the document effecting the suspension or demotion.
46. *Id.*, § .2308(3)(e).
47. G.S. 143-318.11(a)(6).
48. 25 N.C.A.C. 01I, § .2308(4)(f).
49. *Id.*
50. *Id.*
51. *Id.* at (4)(g).
52. *Id.*
53. *Id.*
54. *Id.*
55. *Id.*
56. *Id.*, § .2310(a).
57. G.S. 126-35; 25 N.C.A.C. 01I, § .2310(a).
58. *Id.*
59. *Id.* at (b).
60. G.S. 126-35; 25 N.C.A.C. 01I, § .2310(d).
61. G.S. 126-35; 25 N.C.A.C. 01I, § .2310(d).
62. G.S. 150B-32.
63. G.S. 150B-23(b).
64. *See* G.S. 150B-25; G.S. 150B, §§ 27 (subpoenas), 28 (discovery), 29 (rules of evidence).
65. G.S. 150B-25.1.
66. G.S. 150B-34.
67. G.S. 150B-37.
68. G.S. 150B, §§ 43, 45.
69. G.S. 150B, §§ 45–46.
70. G.S. 150B-51.
71. G.S. 150B-52.
72. 25 N.C.A.C., § .2309(c).
73. *Id.*
74. *Id.*
75. *Id.*
76. G.S. 153A-98.
77. G.S. 153A-98(a).
78. G.S. 153A-98(b).
79. David M. Lawrence, Public Records Law for North Carolina Local Governments ch. 7 (UNC School of Government, 2d ed. 2009).

Chapter 9

The Board's Responsibilities Regarding Social Services Policy and Administration

County social services agencies are subject to a significant amount of state and federal regulation regarding how social services programs are administered. Each county director of social services is responsible for administering and staffing these social services programs at the local level, while complying with a multitude of federal and state requirements for program administration. At the state level, NCDHHS has an important role in developing policy for local agencies, allocating federal and state funding, and exercising oversight over many of these programs. The Social Services Commission also plays a significant role through adopting rules that govern most of the state's social services programs.

The complex legal requirements for operating social services programs, the significant authority granted to the county director of social services, and the role of the state in developing law and policy for social services all leave very little room for county social services boards to make decisions about program administration. Accordingly, county social services boards in North Carolina have relatively limited authority and responsibility regarding social services policy and administration. However, state law does give county social services boards some responsibility and authority to advise local public officials, make certain decisions regarding public assistance programs, monitor and evaluate social services programs, review some social services records, and enter into certain types of contracts. This chapter will discuss those powers and duties of the social services board.

Monitoring and Evaluating Social Services Programs

Under state law, the county social services director and the director's staff, not the county social services board, are primarily responsible for administering public assistance and social services programs for county residents. The board should generally focus on the impact that public assistance and social services programs have on community well-being, not the day-to-day administrative procedures regarding the operation of those programs.

However, even though the county social services board has very little direct authority over social services programs, the board is responsible for consulting with the county social services director regarding problems affecting the department, assisting the director in planning the department's budget, evaluating the director's performance, and disciplining or dismissing the director if necessary.[1] In order to discharge these responsibilities, the social services board must take some level of responsibility for the general oversight of the county DSS as a whole. For example, if the board has reason to suspect that the director is acting in violation of state or federal law with respect to how a program is operated or a service is delivered, the board has a responsibility to investigate the situation and potentially take disciplinary action against the director.

Advising Local Public Officials

State law gives social services boards a responsibility to "advise county and municipal authorities in developing policies and plans to improve the social conditions of the community."[2] This is one of the board's most important responsibilities, but it is often overlooked and ignored. To effectively advise local government officials about social services policies and plans, social services board members must educate themselves about the social and economic issues affecting people in their communities. Board members can advise local officials more effectively when they are familiar with the services and programs offered by the county DSS, as well as health and human services programs administered by other agencies and nonprofit organizations in the community. Understanding the services and programs that are available in the local area will help board members to identify unmet needs in the community, gaps in available funding for social services, and gaps in service delivery to county residents.

Ideally, board members will seek to educate themselves about issues such as unemployment, homelessness and housing insecurity, domestic violence, child abuse and neglect, abuse and neglect of elderly adults and adults with disabilities, hunger and food insecurity, substance-use disorders, and mental health problems. This includes seeking out information about the organizations and agencies that are addressing these problems at the local and state levels, as well as learning about how the county DSS addresses these issues or works with community partners to address them. Through doing this research and talking with community members, board members may learn about the causes of social and economic problems, identify resources that are available (or not available) to solve those problems, and identify the officials and agencies that may have the authority or resources to address these problems. This information will help board members advocate at the local, state, and federal level for the adoption, implementation, and funding of plans and policies to address social and economic problems facing their communities.

Establishing Local Social Services Policies

In addition to the mandated programs that a county social services agency is required to provide under state law, the board of county commissioners (BOCC) has authority to fund additional (nonmandated) county social services programs and attach conditions to the use of county funding for those programs.[3] State law authorizes the county social services board to adopt policies regarding county-funded programs for "the care of indigent persons."[4] The social services board's authority to establish policies for county-funded programs does not extend to mandated state or federal-state social services programs that are only funded *in part* by county tax revenues.

State law technically gives the county social services board authority to establish local policies for the State-County Special Assistance program, the Food and Nutrition Services program, the Foster Care and Adoption Assistance Programs, and other public assistance and social services programs established by Chapter 108A of the North Carolina General Statutes (with the exception of Medicaid).[5] Practically speaking, however, the board's authority to establish policies for these programs is *extremely* limited. The federal and state laws that govern social services programs are highly detailed and comprehensive, meaning there is very little room for the board to make policy decisions about these programs. Federal and state laws and regulations generally dictate these programs' administration, their eligibility criteria, their confidentiality requirements, and the nature, scope, and duration of the assistance and services they provide. Any policy the board adopts regarding these programs must comply with federal and state laws, conform to Social Services Commission rules, and adhere to NCDHHS policies.[6]

Though a county social services board's authority to establish policies for public assistance and social services programs is quite limited, state law and rules do authorize the board to make certain decisions regarding the Work First program, the State-County Special Assistance program, and services funded through the Social Services Block Grant, as described below.

Making Decisions Regarding the State-County Special Assistance Program

The State-County Special Assistance program provides a cash supplement for older adults or adults with disabilities to help pay for room and board in adult care homes, special-care units, or in-home living arrangements. The county social services board is responsible for approving determinations made by the county director of social services about whether to grant assistance to an individual and the amount of assistance to be given.[7] However, the county board of social services may delegate the authority to approve or reject all applications for State-County Special Assistance back to the county DSS director.[8]

Making Decisions Regarding Services Funded Through the Social Services Block Grant

The Social Services Block Grant (SSBG), a major source of federal funding for social services, is a capped entitlement program that provides funding to assist states in delivering social services.[9] SSBG is a flexible funding source that can be used for many different types of social services programs[10] and is the primary source of federal funding for programs such as adult day care and adult protective services. Rules adopted by the Social Services Commission give the county social services board the following responsibilities with respect to SSBG-funded services.

Transportation

The types of transportation that will be provided to people who receive SSBG-funded transportation services, community living services, adult day care services, employment and training support services, and health support services from the county DSS must be documented in the local transportation development plan.[11] In the absence of a local transportation development plan, the county social services board is responsible for documenting and approving the types of transportation the county DSS will make available to people who receive these services.[12] In such a case, the description of the available types of transportation should be documented in the minutes of a social services board meeting, and the minutes should reflect the board's approval of the description.[13] Subject to certain driver qualifications and insurance requirements, transportation services may be provided directly by the county DSS, through purchase of service contracts, by vendor payment, by cash payment to a client, through reimbursement to a client's friend or relative, or through volunteers.[14]

Waiting-List Policy

The county social services board has authority to approve a local waiting-list policy for services funded through the SSBG.[15] Local SSBG waiting-list policies must

1. designate whether the waiting list is used for purposes of meeting prompt provision requirements, to respond to inquiries about services, or both;
2. ensure that all individuals are treated equitably in terms of the manner in which they are advised of the upcoming availability of services;
3. ensure that an individual's name does not remain on the waiting list indefinitely without the individual being notified of the status of the request and the anticipated availability of the service; and
4. designate a reasonable time period, not to exceed ninety days, that an individual's name can remain on the waiting list prior to providing the service or notifying the individual that the service cannot be provided.[16]

Method for Establishing Financial Eligibility

The county board of social services is responsible for determining whether the county social services department will use the declaration or verification method of establishing financial eligibility for SSBG-funded services when eligibility for such services is based on income.[17]

Verification Method

The verification method requires the county DSS to verify an individual's statement as to the individual's eligibility status by obtaining evidence which supports the statement.[18] This evidence may be gathered through reviewing copies of documents, through phone conversations, or by identifying existing DSS records that may confirm the required information.

Declaration Method

Under the declaration method, the individual provides a statement on their status as a public recipient or on the sources and amount of their family's gross income, and the county DSS accepts that statement.[19] However, when the county DSS has reason to believe that the individual's declaration may be inaccurate, it must use the verification method.[20]

Making Decisions Regarding the Work First Program

The federal Temporary Assistance for Needy Families (TANF) program is called "Work First" in North Carolina. Work First focuses on providing eligible families with short-term assistance to help them achieve self-sufficiency through employment.[21] Based on recommendations from NCDHHS, the General Assembly designates each county as either a "standard" county or an "electing" county (described in more detail in Chapter 3).[22] In electing counties, the BOCC must appoint a committee of individuals, including representatives from the county board of social services, to assist in developing the county's Work First plan to respond to community needs.[23]

Social services boards also have the following responsibilities with respect to Work First.

Investigative Assistance

If requested by a district attorney, state law requires county social services boards to provide investigative assistance regarding reports about the abandonment or neglect of certain dependent children, a refusal to support those children, or the misuse of Work First Family Assistance.[24]

Hardship Exemptions from Federal Lifetime Limit

Work First families that include an adult are subject to a sixty-month lifetime limit on the receipt of assistance under the Temporary Assistance for Needy Families (TANF) Block Grant, which includes Work First cash assistance.[25] The sixty-month time limit is a cumulative total and includes the months TANF assistance was received in other states. A family may request a hardship exemption from the sixty-month time limit if the family has experienced circumstances beyond its control that have made leaving the Work First program difficult.[26] The time period of the hardship exemption can extend up to six months.

The county board of social services is responsible for designating a committee to review requests for hardship exemptions. NCDHHS policy recommends that the committee include a Work First case manager, a child-welfare social worker, a vocational-rehabilitation counselor, a Food and Nutrition Services caseworker, a child support agent, and a qualified substance-use-disorder professional.[27] The committee designated by the board of social services must hold "hardship hearings" to approve or deny hardship status to families that have requested exemptions.

Time-Limit Extensions and Appeals

Unless otherwise stated, the material in this section is drawn from the guidelines on federal and state time limits in the NCDHHS *Work First Manual.*[28]

In addition to the sixty-month lifetime limit on receiving TANF assistance, most families in North Carolina that include a work-eligible adult and are receiving Work First employment services are also subject to a twenty-four-month time limit on receiving Work First cash assistance.[29] Electing counties may establish different time limits on cash assistance, so long as they comply with federal time limits.[30] The family may request an appeal when it believes that there are still months remaining on the time limit. If the family agrees that the months on the time clock are correct and wants to ask for additional months of assistance, the family must request an extension.

Extension hearings are held before the county board of social services or its designee. The social services board must maintain confidentiality regarding the extension-hearing process, which means that all extension hearings must be held in closed session.[31] The county must complete the extension-hearing process and issue benefits or send a denial notice within forty-five days from the date of the extension request. The family seeking the extension

- may request information from the case file to help prepare its case for the extension hearing (this does not include confidential information from third parties);
- may choose to attend or not to attend the extension hearing (the family's choice not to attend the extension hearing does not prevent the hearing from being held);

- may delay the extension hearing one time, more than once if the delays are related to the provision of reasonable accommodations;
- may have anyone present at the extension hearing, such as legal counsel obtained at the family's expense;
- may present new information at the hearing, even if it was not previously provided to the county DSS; and
- must provide the information needed to determine the family's current eligibility within ten calendar days of the county's request for information.

Unless it has delegated its authority to hold extension hearings, the social services board must evaluate each case to determine whether the family's net household income meets the income test to be eligible for an extension. The method for these calculations is described in NCDHHS policy.

The social services board may *grant* an extension to an eligible family if it determines that

- the Work First active participant substantially complied with all provisions of the Mutual Responsibility Agreement, considering certain "good cause" exceptions listed in NCDHHS policy (including incapacity, disability, family crisis, or lack of child care, among others); and
- the Work First active participant, through no fault of their own, is unable to obtain or maintain employment that provides a net income of at least the state's maximum Work First payment for the family size.

Conversely, the social services board must *deny* an extension if it determines that the Work First participant

- failed to substantially comply with the Mutual Responsibility Agreement Plan of Action without good cause;
- was dismissed from a job or demoted from a position with cause;
- voluntarily quit a job without good cause; or
- failed to accept a bona fide job offer without good cause.

The county social services board must also determine the length of the extension (anywhere from one to six months) and specify when the extension begins and ends. The board must complete an Extension Hearing Request form (DSS 5301) and return it to the Work First supervisor as soon as possible after reaching a decision. A family may request a state-level appeal if the social services board or its designee denies the family's request for an extension.

Reviewing Cases of Suspected Public Assistance Fraud

State rules give county boards of social services authority to review cases of suspected fraud by applicants or recipients of assistance from Work First, the State-County Special Assistance program, the Crisis Intervention Program (CIP), and the Low-Income Energy Assistance Program (LIEAP).[32] NCDHHS policy also authorizes county boards of social services to review cases of suspected Medicaid fraud.[33] For each of these programs, the board may choose to delegate this authority to the county social services director, if desired.[34]

If the board chooses to delegate its responsibility to review cases of suspected fraud to the director, the delegation should be clearly documented in writing. Since the people on the board and the person filling the director position will change from time to time, having written documentation memorializing any of the board's decisions to delegate its duties helps maintain continuity and role clarity. If the board has not delegated this duty to the county social services director, then the director must present cases of suspected fraud to the board for review. The review process established by state rules and policies differs slightly for different types of public assistance programs, as described below.

Case Review Procedures

Work First, CIP, and LIEAP

If the board has not delegated its duty to review fraud cases for Work First, CIP, or LIEAP, the board must review all cases of suspected fraud in these programs

---

Is Fraud in Public Assistance Programs Common?

If the board chooses to exercise its authority to review fraud cases, board members should be aware that the rates of fraud by recipients of public assistance programs are relatively low. For example, the most recent Congressional Research Report examining SNAP benefits fraud noted that for every 10,000 households participating in SNAP in fiscal year 2016, only about 14 contained a recipient who was investigated and determined to have committed fraud that resulted in an overpayment.[a] During that fiscal year, for every $10,000 in benefits issued to households participating in SNAP, only about $11 were determined by state agencies to have been overpaid due to recipient fraud and were required to be repaid by the overpaid household.[b] The same Congressional Research Report shows that overpayments of SNAP benefits were more likely to arise from an unintentional applicant error during the application process, such as a miscalculation, misunderstanding of SNAP rules, or accidental omission of relevant information.[c]

---

[a] Randy Alison Aussenberg, Cong. Rsch. Serv., R45147, Errors and Fraud in the Supplemental Nutrition Assistance Program (SNAP) (2018).
[b] Id.
[c] Id.

presented to the board by the DSS director.[35] The board must determine whether a person *willfully* and *knowingly* (1) provided incorrect or misleading information in response to oral or written questions; (2) failed to report changes that might have affected the amount of payment; or (3) failed to report the receipt of benefits that the person knew they were not entitled to receive.[36] If the board determines that fraud was the reason for an overpayment of assistance, there must be physical evidence to substantiate that determination.[37]

If the board determines that it suspects fraud, it must instruct the county DSS to (1) seek administrative recoupment, (2) initiate an administrative disqualification hearing or referral for prosecution, (3) pursue civil court action, and/or (4) pursue criminal charges.[38] These options are described in more detail in Title 10A, Chapter 71W, Section .0606(c)(4) of the North Carolina Administrative Code (hereinafter N.C.A.C.).

If the board directs the county DSS to initiate an administrative disqualification hearing, the board must appoint either the DSS director or an impartial county employee to act as the hearings officer.[39] NCDHHS policy recommends that neither investigators nor anyone directly connected with a particular case (for example, the caseworker or the supervisor involved with the case) be designated as the hearings officer.[40]

State-County Special Assistance

If the board has not delegated its duty to review fraud cases for State-County Special Assistance, the board must review all cases of suspected fraud that are presented to the board by the DSS director.[41] The board must determine whether the applicant or recipient *willfully* and *knowingly* (1) misstated or provided incorrect or misleading information in response to oral or written questions; (2) failed to report a change in situation affecting eligibility for the State-County Special Assistance Program or the amount of payment; or (3) failed to report the receipt of payments to which the recipient knew he or she was not entitled.[42]

If the board determines that an applicant or recipient engaged in intentional misrepresentation, it must direct the county DSS to pursue certain administrative actions (as described in 10A N.C.A.C. 71P .0508(e)(2)), civil court action, and/or criminal charges.[43] The state rules also allow the board to direct the county DSS not to pursue any action against the applicant or recipient if there are unusual or hardship circumstances, as set forth in 20 C.F.R. § 404.508(a) and 20 C.F.R. § 416.553(a), in which a payment reduction would deprive the applicant or recipient of necessary income for certain expenses.[44]

Medicaid

The board's role in reviewing certain cases of suspected Medicaid beneficiary fraud is set forth in NCDHHS policies.[45] After an investigation of suspected Medicaid fraud, the investigative summary must be presented to the board of social services or its designee for a decision on whether to refer the case for prosecution or use administrative procedures for collection.[46]

The board or its designee must consider the following factors when deciding what action should be taken regarding the case:[47]

- whether there was a violation of policy;
- whether the violation of policy was against the law;
- whether the elements of criminal action were present; and
- whether a beneficiary willfully and knowingly, with intent to deceive,
    (1) made a false statement or representation,
    (2) failed to disclose a material fact, and as a result,
    (3) obtained, attempted to obtain, or continued to receive Medicaid for the beneficiary or others.

The board or its designee must also consider the following mitigating factors:

- the beneficiary's history of prior and repeat offenses;
- the beneficiary's physical and mental state;
- the recommendation of the district attorney; and
- any other factors pertinent to the case, such as the relevant statutes of limitations on available claims (some claims may be time-barred).

Examining Social Services Records

All information concerning individuals applying for or receiving public assistance or social services that may be directly or indirectly derived from the records, files, or communications of the county DSS or the county board of social services is confidential under state law.[48] Many federal confidentiality laws and regulations also apply to various types of information held by a county DSS.

A state statute, G.S. 108A-11, authorizes county social services board members to examine the county social services department's records regarding applications for and provision of public assistance and social services.[49] However, there are other state and federal confidentiality laws that significantly narrow the board's right of access to records, particularly with respect to child protective services information and certain public assistance information.[50] For example, a 1995 advisory opinion issued by the North Carolina Attorney General's Office concluded that social services board members do not have any right to access child protective services records because these records are subject to provisions of North Carolina's Juvenile Code[51] that do not allow access by governing boards.[52] The county social services director, in consultation with the director's staff or contract attorneys, is responsible for determining which records may be properly inspected by social services board members under state and federal confidentiality laws.

Board members should only use their authority to access social services records to discharge their official board responsibilities. It is unethical for a board member to request or examine records in which the board member has a personal interest, such as records regarding the member's own relatives or friends.[53]

State law prohibits board members from using, disclosing, or publicizing any information regarding individuals applying for or receiving public assistance or social services, including any information a board member may learn through examining social services records.[54]

Approving Social Services Contracts

G.S. 108A-10 authorizes the county social services board to enter into contracts with any public or private agency or individual, under which the county DSS will voluntarily render services to or for the agency or person in exchange for a fee to cover the cost of the services.[55] However, contracts under G.S. 108A-10 are relatively rare. Any fees to be charged by the board using this contract authority must be based on a plan that is developed by the social services director and approved by both the BOCC and the board of social services.

The board has no authority to charge a fee for a particular service if

- charging such a fee is specifically prohibited by statute or regulation,
- the county DSS is required by law to render the service, or
- the recipient of the service is required by law to obtain the service from the county DSS.[56]

Apart from its authority under G.S. 108A-10, an appointed county social services board generally has no legal authority to enter into any type of contract on behalf of the board or the county social services department. Instead, except as otherwise provided by law, the county's authority to enter into contracts must be exercised by the BOCC.[57] As a general rule, all contracts that involve the county, county agencies, or county boards must be approved by the BOCC or a public official designated by the BOCC (such as the county manager, the county purchasing officer, or county department heads). The BOCC could authorize an appointed social services board to approve certain contracts that involve the county DSS. But if the BOCC has not granted such authority, an appointed social services board has no role or responsibility with respect to the approval of contracts other than those made pursuant to G.S. 108A-10.

Likewise, state statutes do not expressly authorize county DSS directors to enter into contracts on behalf of a county DSS. However, the county DSS director may enter into or execute a contract on behalf of the county if authorized to do so under a county ordinance or policy.

Involvement with the Community Child Protection Team

The chair of the county board of social services is required to appoint one social services board member to serve as a member of the county's Community Child Protection Team (CCPT).[58] Each CCPT is responsible for reviewing selected cases involving children who are receiving child protective services from the county DSS and reviewing all cases in which a child has died

- as a result of suspected abuse or neglect within twelve months after the child or the child's family received child protective services or
- within twelve months after a report was made to the social services department regarding the abuse or neglect of the child or another child in the family.[59]

Each CCPT must submit an annual report of recommendations to the BOCC that identifies gaps and deficiencies in the provision of child protective services and that advocates for system improvements and needed resources.[60]

Notes

1. Chapter 108A, Section 9 of the North Carolina General Statutes (hereinafter G.S.).
2. G.S. 108A-9(2).
3. G.S. 153A-255.
4. G.S. 108A-14(4).
5. *See* G.S. 108A-1. Note that Work First is one of the programs established by Chapter 108A. In a county designated by the General Assembly as an "electing" county under G.S. 108A-27.3, the BOCC is authorized to adopt local policies for the county's Work First program. In standard counties, policies are largely determined by NCDHHS through the Standard Work First program. For a description of the differences between "standard" and "electing" counties, please see Chapter 3 of this book.
6. G.S. 108A-1.
7. G.S. 108A-43(a).
8. G.S. 108A-43(a). Directors who have been delegated this authority by their boards are not required to report their actions (regarding approving or rejecting applications) to their boards.
9. *See Social Services Block Grant*, BENEFITS.GOV, https://www.benefits.gov/benefit/775 (last visited Mar. 2, 2023).
10. For a list of services that may be reimbursed with SSBG funds, see Title 10A, Chapter 71R, Section .0101 of the North Carolina Administrative Code (hereinafter N.C.A.C.).
11. 10A N.C.A.C. 71I, § .0101. Per G.S. 136-66.2(b3), each county, with the cooperation of the Department of Transportation, may develop a comprehensive transportation plan. This plan may be adopted by both the BOCC and the Department of Transportation. For portions of a county located within a metropolitan planning organization, the development of a comprehensive transportation plan must take place through that organization.
12. 10A N.C.A.C. 71I, § .0101.
13. *Id.*
14. 10A N.C.A.C. 71I, § .0102.
15. 10A N.C.A.C. 71R, § .0803(b)(1).
16. *Id.,* § .0803(b).
17. *Id.,* § .0701.
18. *Id.,* § .0702.
19. *Id.,* § .0703.
20. *Id.*
21. G.S. 108A-27.
22. G.S. 108A, § 27.2(12)–(14)
23. G.S. 108A-27.3(c).
24. G.S. 15-155.2(a)(1).
25. *See* 45 C.F.R. § 264.1.
26. N.C. DEP'T OF HEALTH & HUM. SERVS., *Federal and State Time Limits, in* WORK FIRST MANUAL, POLICY § 105 (April 1, 2021), https://policies.ncdhhs.gov/divisional/social-services/work-first/policy-manuals/work-first-manual.
27. *Id.*
28. *Id.*
29. G.S. 108A-27.1(a).

30. G.S. 108A-27.1(b).

31. *See* G.S. 143-318.11(a)(1) (authorizing public bodies to hold closed sessions when necessary to prevent the disclosure of information that is privileged or confidential pursuant to state or federal law).

32. *See* 10A N.C.A.C. 71W, § .0606(b) (Work First); 10A N.C.A.C. 71P, § .0508(e) (State-County Special Assistance); 10A N.C.A.C. 71V, § .0107 (LIEAP); 10A N.C.A.C. 71V, § .0204 (CIP).

33. N.C. Dep't of Health & Hum. Servs., Aged, Blind and Disabled Medicaid Manual § MA-2900 (Feb. 9, 2021), https://policies.ncdhhs.gov/divisional/health-benefits-nc-medicaid/adult-medicaid/policies-manuals/ma-2900-recipient-fraud-and-abuse-policy-and-procedures-1; N.C. Dep't of Health & Hum. Servs., Family and Children's Medicaid Manual § MA-3535 (Feb. 10, 2021), https://policies.ncdhhs.gov/divisional/health-benefits-nc-medicaid/family-and-childrens-medicaid/family-and-childrens-medicaid/ma-3535-recipient-fraud-and-abuse-policy-and-procedures.

34. 10A N.C.A.C. 71W, § .0606(b)(3), (c)(1) (Work First); 10A N.C.A.C. 71P, § .0508(d)(2), (e)(1) (State-County Special Assistance). The fraud case review procedures for Work First, including the authority to delegate this responsibility to the director, are incorporated by reference in rules related to LIEAP (10A N.C.A.C. 71V, § .0107) and CIP (10A N.C.A.C. 71V, § .0204).

35. 10A N.C.A.C. 71W, § .0606(b)(3).

36. *Id.* at (2).

37. *Id.* at (3).

38. *Id.* at (4).

39. *Id.* at (4)(B)(II).

40. N.C. Dep't of Health & Hum. Servs., *Fraud and Intentional Program Violations, in* Work First Manual, Policy § 207 (Apr. 1, 2002), https://policies.ncdhhs.gov/divisional/social-services/work-first/policy-manuals/work-first-manual.

41. 10A N.C.A.C. 71P, § .0508(e)(1).

42. *Id.*

43. *Id.* at (2).

44. *Id.* at (2)(D).

45. N.C. Dep't of Health & Hum. Servs., Aged, Blind and Disabled Medicaid Manual, *supra* note 33; N.C. Dept. of Health and Hum. Servs., Family and Children's Medicaid Manual, *supra* note 33.

46. *Id.*

47. *Id.*

48. G.S. 108A-80(a).

49. G.S. 108A-11.

50. For more analysis on this topic, see Aimee Wall, *Access to Confidential Client Records by Social Services Governing Boards,* Coates' Canons: NC Loc. Gov't L. (blog) (UNC School of Government, Apr. 26, 2016), https://canons.sog.unc.edu/2016/04/access-confidential-records-social-services-governing-boards/.

51. The Juvenile Code is found in Chapter 7B of the North Carolina General Statutes. Provisions in the Juvenile Code that restrict the disclosure of child-protective-services records include G.S. 7B-302(a1) and G.S. 7B-2901.

52. N.C. Dep't of Justice, Office of the Att'y Gen., Advisory Opinion: Access to Records by Social Services Boards, Op. N.C. Att'y Gen. (Apr. 20, 1995), https://ncdoj.gov/opinions/access-to-records-by-social-services-board/.

53. *Id.* ("A social services board member who examines and reviews files in which he has a personal interest places himself in conflict with his public duties. He is in effect serving two masters, i.e., himself and the public. This is unethical and serves to undermine the public's trust in its officials.").

54. G.S. 108A, §§ 11, 80.
55. The language of the statute refers to "the board of social services agree[ing] to render services," but this statute has historically been interpreted as applying to contracts for services that will be voluntarily provided by the county department of social services (not the board itself). The legislative history for H.B. 66 (Session 1979), which originally enacted this statute, shows that the General Assembly's intention was to allow county departments of social services to charge fees for certain services in a similar fashion to local health departments.
56. Social Services, Adoptions, Fees for Services by County Departments of Social Services, Op. N.C. Atty. Gen., 1984 WL 182160 (Office of the N.C. Att'y Gen. Jan. 26, 1984).
57. G.S. 153A-11.
58. G.S. 7B-1407(b)(6).
59. G.S. 7B-1406(a)(1).
60. G.S. 7B-1406(a)(2).

Chapter 10

The Budgeting Process for Departments of Social Services

Each appointed county social services board is responsible for helping the county director of social services plan the proposed annual budget for the county DSS.[1] To carry out this responsibility, social services board members should understand the funding streams for the DSS in their county and the basic steps in the DSS's budgeting process.

Social services financing is complicated by a complex interplay of federal, state, and county funding. The federal government plays a major role in financing many social services programs. Those programs contribute many federal and state dollars to local economies, but they also require the expenditure of substantial county funds. In some cases, the North Carolina General Assembly assigns responsibility to the counties for a portion of the nonfederal cost of certain federally funded programs. In other cases, county expenditures are required as a condition of receiving other federal and state funds for social services. Additionally, counties may need to spend county funds to provide services and programs for which state and federal funds are either unavailable or insufficient.

Federal Funding for Social Services

All federal funding for social services comes with certain strings (conditions) attached, meaning that recipients of these funds must comply with certain legal requirements. Among other things, these legal requirements may specify who is eligible for assistance under a given program, what types of assistance and services

---

This chapter incorporates material about social services funding and the budgeting process from Aimee N. Wall, *Social Services, in* COUNTY AND MUNICIPAL GOVERNMENT IN NORTH CAROLINA 677–88 (Frayda S. Bluestein ed., UNC School of Government, 2d ed. 2014) and John L. Saxon, SOCIAL SERVICES IN NORTH CAROLINA (UNC School of Government, 2009), 203–18.

may be provided, how much assistance may be provided, how long assistance may be provided, when confidential program information may be disclosed, and how much states (or, in North Carolina, state and local governments) must contribute to the cost of these programs.

Federal funding constitutes a significant portion of all social services expenditures in North Carolina. For state fiscal year 2023–2034, NCDHHS estimates that the federal government will fund 83.97 percent of total statewide costs for public assistance programs, program assistance administration, and services programs.[2] In that same budget estimate, counties are projected to provide 12.35 percent of total costs, while the state is projected to provide 3.67 percent of total costs.

Some federally funded public assistance programs, such as Food and Nutrition Services (FNS) and Medicaid, are known as *entitlement programs*, meaning that benefits must be provided to every person who applies and meets the program's eligibility requirements. Regardless of how many people qualify for benefits under an entitlement program, the federal government must provide funds sufficient to pay the federal share of benefits for all eligible individuals.

The mix of federal, state, and county funding varies for each entitlement program. In the FNS program, the federal government pays the full cost of the direct benefits, but only part of the costs to administer the program.[3] For state fiscal year 2023–2024, NCDHHS estimates that federal funding will provide over two billion dollars in FNS benefits (100% of costs) and over 111 million dollars for FNS program administration (50% of costs), while counties will fund the remaining 50 percent of FNS program administration costs.[4] In the Medicaid program, the state has an open-ended obligation to provide funds sufficient to pay the nonfederal share of Medicaid-coverage costs for all eligible individuals.[5] While federal and state government bear the vast majority of Medicaid-related costs, counties do provide some funds to pay the nonfederal share of program administration costs. For state fiscal year 2023–2024, NCDHHS estimates that counties will provide almost 104 million in Medicaid program administration funding (almost 29% of costs) while the federal government will cover over 71 percent of administrative costs.[6]

In other programs, such as Work First, the Low-Income Energy Assistance Program (LIEAP), and most service programs, the amount of federal funding is capped. Federal appropriations provide a fixed amount of funding, often called a *block grant*. In order to receive these funds, state and local governments must contribute either a specified percentage of "matching" funds or an amount representing a "maintenance of effort" tied to amounts expended or budgeted for the program in a designated prior period. The state must develop comprehensive state plans describing the proposed use of the federal block grant funds and related state and local funds. The General Assembly is responsible for approving the distribution of federal block grant funds to counties.

If the federal funds and the required state and local contributions are insufficient to provide benefits or services to everyone who is eligible for a particular program, the state or local government must either limit the number of people served by the program, limit the amount of benefits or the level of services provided, or provide additional state or local funding for the program. In some cases, the ability to limit eligibility, benefits, or services may be constrained by program requirements associated with federal funds.

State and County Funding for Social Services

The General Assembly has the authority to decide whether and how to divide the nonfederal share of costs for social services programs between the state and counties.[7] North Carolina generally requires counties to pay the bulk of the nonfederal share of administrative costs for public assistance programs, as well as a significant portion of the cost of social services provided to county residents.[8]

Every board of county commissioners (BOCC) is required to levy and collect taxes sufficient to meet its county's share of expenses for mandated social services programs.[9] If a county does not pay or arrange for payment of its full share of the costs, the state budget director is authorized to withhold from the county any state appropriations for public assistance and related administrative costs or to direct the secretary of revenue and the state controller to withhold specified tax revenues owed to the county. The state budget director must notify the chair of the BOCC of the proposed action prior to withholding any funds. [10]

The BOCC has discretion as to how much county money (if any) to budget for *nonmandated* social services programs.[11]

In some instances, counties must fill a funding gap with county funds to fulfill a legal mandate that is unfunded or underfunded by state and federal funds. For example, state law requires county departments of social services to provide adult protective services, but there is very little state or federal funding available for such services. In order to fulfill the legal mandate to protect vulnerable adults, a BOCC must appropriate county funds to support a county DSS's provision of adult protective services. Likewise, federal and state funding are sometimes inadequate to support a sufficient number of social workers and attorneys to handle all the child welfare cases in a given county, in which case the county must "fill the gap" in services for these children with county funds.

Funding Estimates for County Social Services Agencies

Before February 15 of each year, NCDHHS is required to notify the county social services director, the director of public health, the county manager, and the BOCC of the amount of state and federal funds estimated to be available to the county for public assistance, social services, and public health programs and related administrative costs for the next fiscal year.[12] The notice states the percentage of county financial participation expected to be required for each program. Periodically, the state revises these estimates to reflect new state-budget figures and actions taken by the General Assembly, Congress, and federal agencies. Accordingly, the budgeting process for county social services agencies involves some degree of uncertainty regarding the exact amount of county funds that will be needed to fund a county's share of the cost of mandated programs.

County social services budgets generally estimate expenditures that are higher than the amounts indicated in NCDHHS's estimates. These higher county-level estimates are often due to needing to fill a funding gap, as described above. For example, federal and state funds available to the county for child protective services, along with NCDHHS's estimate of the county's match, may be insufficient to hire the number of social workers necessary to carry out the county's legal responsibility to provide protective services to abused and neglected children. In other cases, counties may need to spend additional funds to comply with state mandates that are not accompanied by state funding. Additionally, counties may want to provide nonmandated social services programs to meet unique local needs. Those optional, nonmandated programs and services are not reflected in NCDHHS's budget estimates and must be supported by county funds if other federal and state funding is not available.

The Budgeting Process for a County Social Services Agency

The Local Government Budget and Fiscal Control Act (LGBFCA)[13] governs the budgeting, expenditure, and accounting of all money received or spent by local government agencies, including county social services departments and consolidated human services agencies. Under the LGBFCA, local government agencies that are not independent units of local government or public authorities must have their budgeting, disbursing, and accounting done for them by the unit of local government of which they are a part (i.e., the county). Though the county social services director is responsible for administering funds allocated to social services,[14] the budget for a county social services agency is part of the county budget, and the expenditure of money by a county social services agency is subject to oversight by the county. State law requires that all county expenditures—including those made by a county social services department—be made in accordance with the LGBFCA.[15]

The county social services director is responsible, with the assistance of the county social services board, for planning the proposed budget for the county social services department.[16] Under the LGBFCA, the county DSS director must submit the department's proposed budget to the county budget officer no later than April 30 (or an earlier date fixed by the county budget officer).[17] The same requirements apply to a consolidated human services agency, except that the consolidated human services director is the individual responsible for planning and submitting the agency's budget, with the assistance of the consolidated human services board.[18]

The department's proposed budget must include a request for appropriations for the coming fiscal year, an estimate of departmental revenues for the coming year (including federal, state, and nonpublic funding), actual and estimated expenditures for each category of expenditure included in the county budget ordinance for the current and immediately preceding fiscal years, actual and estimated amounts realized for each source of revenue for the current and immediately preceding fiscal years, and any additional information requested by the budget officer.[19]

The LGBFCA requires the county budget officer to prepare a proposed budget for the county (including the county DSS) and submit it to the BOCC by June 1.[20] The budget officer's proposed budget may increase, decrease, or revise the budget submitted by the county DSS director without the approval or consent of the DSS director. After the proposed county budget is submitted to the BOCC, the county commissioners must hold a public hearing on the proposed budget.[21] Following the hearing, but no later than July 1,[22] the BOCC must adopt a balanced[23] budget ordinance that accepts or modifies the manager's proposed budget; makes appropriations of county revenues for specified purposes, functions, activities, or objectives;[24] appropriates sufficient funds to pay the county's share of mandated public assistance and social services programs;[25] levies the county property tax for the coming fiscal year;[26] and includes the county's estimated revenues for the coming fiscal year.[27]

The Role of the Social Services Board in Social Services Funding

As described above, each appointed county social services board is responsible for helping the county director of social services plan the proposed annual budget for the county DSS.[28] However, an appointed county social services board does not have the legal authority to approve or disapprove the county's social services budget, to determine the size of the budget, to levy the local taxes or provide the funding that will be used to provide social services, or to administer the county's social services budget.

An appointed county social services board should work with the social services director, the county manager, the county commissioners, other state and local government officials, and the community to confirm whether adequate funding is available for the public assistance and social services programs that county residents need. One of a social services board's statutory duties is to "advise county and municipal authorities in developing policies and plans to improve the social conditions of the community."[29] Among other things, this responsibility may include advocating for sufficient funding for the county department of social services.

Learning about the various funding streams for social services programs is an important part of your role as a member of the governing board for a county social services agency. Understanding the limitations on funding will help you assist the director in planning the agency budget and identify gaps in federal and state funding that need to be filled to meet the unique needs in your community.

Notes

1. Chapter 108A, Section 9(3) of the North Carolina General Statutes (hereinafter G.S.).
2. *See* N.C. Dep't of Health & Hum. Servs., *County Budget Estimates State Totals—State Fiscal Year 2023–2024*, https://www.ncdhhs.gov/divisions/social-services/county-staff-information/budget-information/dss-budget-estimates (under the heading County Budget Estimates 2023-2024, select Budget Estimates State Totals to access PDF).
3. *See generally* 7 U.S.C. §§ 2014(a), 2025.
4. *See* N.C. Dep't of Health & Hum. Servs., *supra* note 2.
5. *See generally* 42 U.S.C. § 1396b.
6. *See* N.C. Dep't of Health & Hum. Servs., *supra* note 2.
7. G.S. 108A-87.
8. *See* N.C. Dep't of Health & Hum. Servs., *supra* note 2.
9. G.S. 108A-90.
10. G.S. 108A-93.
11. *See* G.S. 153A-255 (giving each county the authority to "undertake, sponsor, organize, engage in, and support . . . social service programs intended to further the health, welfare, education, employment, safety, comfort, and convenience of its citizens").
12. G.S. 108A-88.
13. G.S. 159, art. 3.
14. *See* G.S. 108A-4.
15. *See generally* G.S. 159, §§ 8(a), 28.
16. G.S. 108A-9(3).
17. G.S. 159-10. In counties having the manager form of government, the county manager is the statutory budget officer. *See* G.S. 159-9. However, in some counties, a budget director who reports to the manager (or occasionally to the finance officer) actually performs most of the day-to-day duties of the budget officer.
18. G.S. 153A, § 77(d)(7), (e)(5).
19. G.S. 159-10.
20. G.S. 159-11(b).
21. G.S. 159-12(b).
22. G.S. 159-13(a).
23. G.S. 159-8(a).
24. G.S. 159-7(b)(2).
25. G.S. 108A-90.
26. G.S. 159, § 7(b)(2), 13(c).
27. G.S. 159, § 13(a), (b)(7).
28. G.S. 108A-9(3).
29. G.S. 108A-9(2).

Chapter 11

The Role of the Board of County Commissioners in Social Services

Regardless of a county's agency structure for social services, the board of county commissioners (BOCC) has some level of involvement with the county's governing board for social services.

As of the publication of this book, the BOCC serves as the governing board for social services in twenty-five North Carolina counties. In some of those counties, the BOCC is governing a consolidated human services agency (CHSA) that includes social services, while in others, the BOCC is governing a standalone county DSS. Direct county commissioner governance of social services agencies is discussed later in this chapter.

In counties with appointed social services boards governing a county DSS, the BOCC has authority to appoint either one or two members of the social services board (depending on whether the board has three or five members). A county commissioner often serves as a member of the appointed social services board.

In counties with appointed consolidated human services (CHS) boards governing a CHSA, the BOCC has authority to appoint all of the governing-board members.

No matter what social services governance structure is in place, every BOCC has a number of important powers and responsibilities related to social services, which are discussed later in this chapter.

Direct County Commissioner Governance of County Social Services Agencies

A BOCC can directly assume the powers and duties of a governing board appointed by the BOCC or acting under and pursuant to the authority of the BOCC.[1] In the human services arena, such boards include a county board of health, county board of social services, or CHS board. A BOCC cannot abolish and assume the powers and duties of a board for a multicounty agency, such as a regional board of social services or a district board of health.[2]

If the BOCC plans to serve as the governing board for a county DSS or a CHSA, it must first hold a public hearing.[3] The BOCC must give thirty days' notice of the public hearing in a newspaper having general circulation in the county, and it must adhere to any notice requirements that would generally apply to official meetings of the BOCC under North Carolina's open meetings law.[4] The hearing requirement is triggered by the BOCC assuming the powers and duties of another board, which could be a local board of health, a county board of social services, or a CHS board. Following the public hearing, the BOCC may adopt a resolution "assuming and conferring upon the board of county commissioners all powers, responsibilities and duties" of the governing board for social services.[5]

If a BOCC decides to assume the powers and duties of a CHS board in a county where the CHSA includes public health, the BOCC must appoint an advisory committee for public health.[6] The advisory committee must, at a minimum, include members representing all of the required categories of membership for a county board of health, which are found in Chapter 130A, Section 35 of the North Carolina General Statutes.[7] There is no corresponding legal requirement to create a social services advisory committee when the BOCC assumes the powers and duties of a social services governing board. However, a BOCC has the *option* of appointing an advisory committee for social services. The BOCC could either expand the public health advisory committee to include members with social services expertise or appoint a separate advisory committee for social services, but neither option is required by law.[8]

A BOCC that abolishes the governing board for social services takes on all the responsibilities of the social services board, including the responsibilities related to social services policy and administration described in Chapter 9. If the BOCC is governing a county DSS, this includes the responsibility to recruit, hire, evaluate, discipline, and dismiss the county DSS director, as described in Chapters 7 and 8.

Serving Ex Officio on an Appointed Board of Social Services or CHS Board

In counties with an appointed social services board, the BOCC often appoints one of its own members to serve on the board to help foster communication between the two public bodies (though it is not required to do so). In counties with an appointed CHS board, the BOCC is *required* to appoint a county commissioner to be on the board.[9]

When the BOCC appoints a county commissioner to serve on the county's board of social services or a CHS board, it is an *ex officio* appointment.[10] This means that a county commissioner is considered to be serving on the social services board as a part of the commissioner's duties as a BOCC member and not as a separate public office. Accordingly, the county commissioner's ex officio service on the social services board does not "count" as a separate public office for purposes of the multiple-office-holding limit described in Chapter 5.

The term of a county commissioner who serves ex officio on an appointed county board of social services is the same as other board members and is not tied to or affected by the commissioner's term on the BOCC.[11] However, a county commissioner who serves ex officio on an appointed CHS board may only serve on the board for as long as the member is a county commissioner.[12]

Responsibilities of all BOCCs Regarding Social Services

Even in counties where the BOCC does not serve directly as the governing board for social services, the BOCC has many duties regarding the local social services agency, board, and programs.

Duties Related to Organization and Governance of the County Social Services Agency

The BOCC is responsible for determining (1) the type of agency that will provide social services in the county and (2) the type of governing board for that agency. These options are described in Chapters 1 and 2.

In a county with an appointed county board of social services, the BOCC determines whether the board should consist of three or five members.[13]

The BOCC is responsible for appointing one member of a three-member board of social services or two members of a five-member board of social services.[14] Many BOCCs appoint one of their own members to serve on the social services board, but the BOCC is not *required* to appoint one of its own members to the social services board. For more information on appointment schedules, procedures, and limitations, please refer to Chapter 5.

Duties Related to Funding, Fees, and Compensation

A primary role of the BOCC is ensuring the adequacy of funds for social services programs in the county budget. That role is discussed in Chapter 10.

The BOCC has authority to establish per diem rates and a policy for subsistence and travel reimbursement for social services board members.[15] If the BOCC establishes a per diem rate and a policy for reimbursement, it will also need to include funds in the county budget to cover such expenses.

State law authorizes the county social services board to enter into contracts under which the county DSS will voluntarily render services in exchange for a fee (see Chapter 9).[16] Any fees charged by the board using this contract authority must be based on a plan that is developed by the social services director and approved by the BOCC and the board of social services. The board of social services is required to make an annual report to the county commissioners regarding receipt of such fees.

In a county with a DSS, the BOCC is responsible for approving the DSS director's salary.[17] In a county with an appointed board of social services, the board and the BOCC should make every effort to reach agreement on the salary amount, but the BOCC has the final authority to accept or reject the social services board's recommendation.

Duties Related to Social Services Programs and Administration

Through its power over the county budget, the BOCC has authority to determine what *nonmandated* public assistance programs or services the county will provide. State law requires counties to participate in a number of social services programs but also authorizes counties to "undertake, sponsor, organize, engage in, and support other social services programs intended to further the health, welfare, education, safety, comfort, and convenience of its citizens."[18] Many counties, for example, provide some form of general assistance to help address emergency needs of people not eligible for other benefits.

State law allows the BOCC, with the approval of the county social services board, to appoint an attorney as the "special county attorney for social services" or to designate a county attorney to serve in that role.[19] A county is not required to have a special county attorney for social services, but if it does, that attorney's duties include serving as legal adviser to the BOCC, the director of social services, and the social services governing board regarding social services matters.[20] The BOCC is also responsible for determining the attorney's compensation.[21]

State law requires counties to operate the State-County Special Assistance program, which is designed to assist needy aged or disabled persons in paying for room and board in adult care homes, special-care units, and in-home living arrangements. The BOCC has authority to determine whether this program will also provide financial assistance for a different category of "certain disabled persons" who are in private living arrangements but may not otherwise qualify for State-County Special Assistance under the eligibility requirements set forth in state law.[22]

Each county must administer a child support enforcement program.[23] Most county child support enforcement programs are operated by the county DSS. However, each BOCC has the option of creating an independent county department for child support enforcement, locating the program in another county department or office, or contracting with a private entity or another county to operate the program.[24]

Duties Related to the Work First Program

State law allows each BOCC to indicate to NCDHHS whether the county wants to be a "standard" or "electing" county for purposes of the Work First program (see Chapter 3 for a description of Work First).[25] In a standard county, NCDHHS is responsible for the development and supervision of the Work First program, which is administered by the county DSS.[26] In an electing county, the BOCC is directly responsible for the development, administration, and implementation of the Work

First program.[27] A board's request to be an electing county must be supported by a three-fifths vote by the commissioners. The General Assembly designates each county as either a standard county or an electing county based on recommendations from NCDHHS.[28]

An electing county has more authority to set eligibility criteria, payment levels, and other program features that the state sets for standard counties.[29] In an electing county, the BOCC is responsible for

- establishing outcome and performance goals,
- establishing eligibility criteria,
- entering into Mutual Responsibility Agreements with Work First recipients,
- ensuring that services and resources are available to help participants comply with the agreements,
- monitoring compliance with those agreements,
- ensuring that participants engage in the required hours of work activities,
- developing and submitting to NCDHHS a biennial county Work First plan,
- developing and implementing an appeals process for the county's Work First program, and
- complying with all state and federal laws regarding the Work First program.[30]

A BOCC may delegate most of these responsibilities to other public or private entities, but the BOCC ultimately remains accountable for all of them.[31]

In electing counties, the BOCC must appoint a committee of individuals to identify the needs of the population to be served by Work First and to assist in developing the county's Work First plan to respond to those needs.[32] The committee membership must include, but is not limited to, individuals from the county board of social services, the board of the area mental health authority, the local board of health, the local school systems, the business community, the BOCC, and the community-based organizations representative of the population served by the Work First program.[33]

NCDHHS policy also requires standard counties to establish a committee for the biennial Work First planning process and establishes membership requirements for that committee.[34]

Notes

1. Chapter 153A, Section 77(a) of the North Carolina General Statutes (hereinafter G.S.). Exceptions to this rule are stated in G.S. 153A-76.
2. G.S. 153A-76.
3. G.S. 153A-77(a).
4. *Id.; see generally* G.S. 143-318.12 (public notice requirements for official meetings of public bodies).
5. G.S. 153A-77(a).
6. The requirement for a health advisory committee applies only to counties that abolish their health boards after January 1, 2012. This amounts to an exception for Mecklenburg County, which abolished its health boards (a county board of health, and subsequently a CHS board) before that date.
7. This means that the advisory committee must include one physician licensed to practice medicine in North Carolina, one licensed dentist, one licensed optometrist, one licensed veterinarian, one registered nurse, one licensed pharmacist, one county commissioner, one professional engineer, and three representatives of the general public. All the members must be residents of the county where the agency is located.
8. *See* G.S. 153A-77(a).
9. G.S. 153A-77(c).
10. G.S. 128-1.2. Ex officio appointments are discussed in greater detail in A. Fleming Bell, II, Ethics, Conflicts, and Offices: A Guide for Local Officials (UNC School of Government, 2d ed. 2010).
11. *See* State *ex rel.* Pitts v. Williams, 260 N.C. 168 (1963); G.S. 108A-4 (terms for social services board members); *see also* John L. Saxon, *Stay or Go? County Commissioners on Social Services Boards,* Popular Gov't, Winter 2000, at 27, 30–31.
12. G.S. 153A-77(c).
13. G.S. 108A-2.
14. G.S. 108A-3.
15. G.S. 108A-8.
16. G.S. 108A-10.
17. G.S. 108A-13.
18. G.S. 153A-255.
19. G.S. 108A-16.
20. G.S. 108A-15.
21. G.S. 108A-17.
22. Per G.S. 108A-42, a "Certain Disabled" person is a person in a private living arrangement who is at least eighteen but younger than sixty-five, "having a physical or mental impairment which substantially precludes him from obtaining gainful employment, which impairment appears reasonably certain to continue without substantial improvement throughout his lifetime." By contrast, eligibility for State-County Special Assistance requires that the recipient meet certain income criteria, along with being (1) sixty-five years of age or older or (2) between the ages of eighteen and sixty-five and *permanently and totally* disabled or legally blind. G.S. 108A-41. Eligibility requirements for the "Certain Disabled Program" are set forth at Title 10A, Chapter 71P, Section .080 of the North Carolina Administrative Code.
23. G.S. 110-141.

24. *Id.* Until 2010, about one-third of North Carolina counties chose to have the state operate their child support enforcement programs. That option was eliminated effective July 1, 2010, and now all counties must have their own programs. S.L. 2009-451, § 10.46A(a).
25. G.S. 108A-27(e). When notifying NCDHHS of the county's desire to be designated as electing or standard, the county must submit documentation demonstrating that three-fifths of its county commissioners support the desired designation.
26. G.S. 108A-27.8(a).
27. G.S. 108A-27(f).
28. G.S. 108A, § 27.2(12)–(14).
29. *Compare* G.S. 108A-27.3 (duties of electing counties) *with* G.S. 108A-27.6 (duties of standard counties).
30. G.S. 108A-27.3.
31. G.S. 108A-27.3(b).
32. G.S. 108A-27.3(c).
33. G.S. 108A-27.3(c).
34. *See* N.C. Dep't of Health & Hum. Servs., *The Planning Process for Work First, in* Work First Manual, Policy § 003 (July 1, 2011), https://policies.ncdhhs.gov/divisional/social-services/work-first/policy-manuals/work-first-manual.

Chapter 12

Ethical Standards and Legal Prohibitions for Social Services Board Members

As used in this book, the term *ethics* refers broadly to standards of behavior that the public expects from people who hold public office.[1] When discussing ethical standards related to board service, it is important to distinguish between conduct that is legally prohibited and conduct that merely falls short of ethical norms.

Some conduct by public officials may violate state or federal laws. That conduct is both *unethical* and *illegal*. Other conduct by social services board members may violate ethical norms but not actually violate any laws. In other words, that behavior would be *unethical* but not *illegal*.

Board members should not engage in unethical behavior, regardless of whether the behavior violates the law. For purposes of clarity, this chapter will attempt to distinguish between ethical expectations and legal prohibitions.

Ethical Expectations for Public Officials

Basic Standards of Ethical Behavior

The general public expects all public officials, including county social services board members, to act ethically in their public and private lives. Based on basic ethical principles, social services board members should

- devote adequate time and energy to their board responsibilities;
- make fair, impartial decisions;
- act in the public interest and for the public good;
- not use their offices to benefit themselves, their family members, or their friends;
- exercise sound judgment and discretion in connection with their official duties; and
- act honestly, courteously, and collaboratively when working together as a board.

Conflicts of Interest

The term *conflict of interest* generally refers to a conflict between an individual's personal, family, business, professional, or financial interests and that individual's role, responsibilities, duties, or actions as a public official.[2] Put another way, a conflict of interest occurs when an individual's private interests interfere (or may interfere) with that individual's independence, decision-making, and judgement as a board member.

County social services board members should act in the public interest—not for their own personal benefit—when serving as public officials. They should take reasonable actions to avoid actual and potential conflicts between their personal interests and public responsibilities. When possible, board members should avoid even the *appearance* of acting unethically, inappropriately, or for their own benefit.[3] Avoiding conflicts of interest helps the board to maintain the public's trust.

If the conflict between an individual's personal interests and professional responsibilities as a social services board member is significant and unavoidable, it may constitute good cause for requesting the board member's resignation or, if the board member fails to resign, removing the member from the board. More information about removal of board members may be found in Chapter 5.

In some cases, making or administering certain contracts (or attempting to influence someone who does) when a board member has a conflict of interest is not only unethical but also illegal. The laws related to conflicts of interest in contracting will be discussed later in this chapter.

Political Activities

Social services board members should not use their positions on the board to promote political candidates, parties, or platforms. The social services board should be seen by the public as a nonpartisan, politically neutral entity. When board members use their positions on the board to promote political parties or candidates, it can cause members of the public to lose trust in the board's motives and impartiality.

Legally Prohibited Conduct

Involvement with Contracts for Personal Benefit

Chapter 14, Section 234 of the North Carolina General Statutes (hereinafter G.S.) addresses conflicts of interest related to contracts. Specifically, this law prohibits public officials, including county social services board members, from the following actions.

- *Prohibition 1:* A board member is prohibited from receiving a direct benefit from a public contract if the board member is involved in *making or administering* the contract.[4]
- *Prohibition 2:* A board member is prohibited from *influencing or attempting to influence* any person involved in making or administering a public contract if the board member will derive a direct benefit from the contract.[5]

- *Prohibition 3:* A board member is prohibited from soliciting or receiving "any gift, favor, reward, service, or promise of reward, including a promise of future employment, in exchange for *recommending, influencing, or attempting to influence* the award of a contract" by the county.[6]

Violating any one of these conflict-of-interest provisions in G.S. 14-234 is a criminal offense (a Class 1 misdemeanor).[7] Moreover, contracts made in violation of the statute are void.[8]

What Is a "Direct Benefit"?

A board member directly benefits from a public contract if the board member or the board member's spouse "(i) has more than a ten percent (10%) ownership or other interest in an entity that is a party to the contract; (ii) derives any income or commission directly from the contract; or (iii) acquires property under the contract."[9]

This means that Prohibitions 1 and 2 relate not only to contracts that may benefit the board member, but also to contracts that may benefit the board member's spouse.

What Does It Mean to "Make or Administer" a Contract?

A public official who "participates in the development of specifications or terms or in the preparation or award of the contract" or who is a member of a board that takes action with respect to the contract (regardless of whether the official participates in the action) is involved in *making* a contract.[10] A public official who "oversees the performance of [a] contract or has authority to make decisions regarding the contract or to interpret the contract" is involved in *administering* a contract.[11]

Appointed social services boards have no general legal authority to make or administer contracts involving the county DSS, so they are rarely involved in making or administering public contracts (see Chapter 9). As a result, Prohibition 1 (described earlier) will rarely apply to county social services board members. It is more common for board members to run afoul of Prohibition 2 or 3, which involve improperly influencing someone else (such as the DSS director or a county commissioner)[12] who is involved in making or administering a contract.

Are There Any Exceptions to These Prohibitions Around Contracts?

There are a number of exceptions to Prohibition 1, in which a board member is prohibited from deriving a direct benefit from a contract that the board member is involved in making or administering.[13]

For example, Prohibition 1 does not apply to an employment relationship between the county social services department and the spouse of a county social services board member if the board member

1. does not participate in deliberating or voting with respect to the making or administering of the contract and
2. does not attempt to influence any other person (such as the DSS director) who is involved in making or administering the contract.[14]

Prohibition 1 also does not apply to a contract involving payment to a county social services board member or the board member's spouse for services, facilities, or supplies furnished directly to "needy" individuals under any federal or state social services program if

1. the program is open generally to all providers of services on a nondiscriminatory basis;
2. neither the county social services department nor its agents and employees have any control over the selection of participating providers by beneficiaries of the program;
3. the payment for services, facilities, or supplies is in the same amount as would be paid to any other participating provider;
4. the board member does not participate in approving the payment;
5. the board member does not deliberate or vote on the contract; and
6. the board member does not attempt to influence any other person (such as the DSS director) who is involved in making or administering the contract.[15]

There is also a "small jurisdiction" exception to Prohibition 1 for contracts benefitting some individuals on the social services board. Specifically, this exception applies to a board member who is a physician, pharmacist, dentist, optometrist, veterinarian, or nurse serving on a social services board in a county where there is no village, town, or city with a population of more than 20,000 people.[16] If a contract provides a direct benefit to a board member who fits that description, the board may still make or administer the contract so long as

1. the contract (or series of contracts) "is approved by specific resolution of the [social services board] adopted in an open and public meeting, and recorded in its minutes";
2. the amount of the contract "does not exceed twenty thousand dollars ($20,000) for medically related services [or] sixty thousand dollars ($60,000) for other goods or services within a 12-month period";
3. the board member entering into the contract does not participate in any way or vote;
4. the total annual amount of contracts with the board member is "specifically noted in the audited annual financial statement of the village, town, city, or county"; and
5. the social services board posts "in a conspicuous place in its village, town, or city hall, or courthouse" (e.g., the door of its regular meeting room), "a list of all such officials with whom such contracts have been made," briefly describing the subject matter of the contracts and showing their total amounts (covering the preceding twelve months and updated at least quarterly).[17]

This exception recognizes the reality that in some less populated counties, a medical or dental professional serving on the social services board may be the only person available (or one of few) in the county to provide certain necessary services.

Key Takeaways

Learning about the prohibitions in G.S. 14-234 and the exceptions to those prohibitions can feel confusing. Here are some key takeaways to remember:

- Board members should never, under any circumstances, attempt to influence the county DSS director or any other public official or employee involved in making or administering a contract if the board member or board member's spouse will receive a direct benefit from the contract.
- Board members should never, under any circumstances, attempt to influence the county DSS director or any other public official or employee involved in making or administering a contract in exchange for any gift, favor, reward, service, or promise of reward (regardless of whether the board member receives any direct benefit under the contract).
- If a board member is involved in any way in making decisions about a contract or overseeing the performance of a contract, and the board member knows that the contract may provide a benefit to the board member or the board member's spouse, then the board member should take a step back and consult with the county attorney prior to taking any action with respect to the contract. The county attorney or other legal counsel will be able to help determine whether the board member's involvement with the contract is permitted under one of the exceptions in the law.

Accepting Gifts and Favors

Another North Carolina statute, G.S. 133-32, makes it a Class 1 misdemeanor for certain public officials and government employees to willfully receive or accept a gift or favor from a contractor, subcontractor, or supplier who has a contract with a governmental agency, has performed under such a contract within the past year, or anticipates bidding on one in the future.[18] Specifically, this prohibition on receiving or accepting gifts or favors applies to any social services board member, DSS director, or DSS employee who is involved in (1) preparing plans, specifications, or estimates for public contracts; (2) awarding or administering public contracts; or (3) inspecting or supervising construction.[19]

This statute does not prohibit public officials or government employees from receiving customary gifts or favors from friends and family members, so long as it is clear that the gifts are motivated by preexisting friendships or familial relationships rather than by a desire to do business with a government agency.[20] Likewise, the statute contains exceptions for honorariums, advertising items of nominal value, meals at banquets, donations to professional organizations to defray meeting expenses, and participation in functions at meetings of professional organizations that are available to all attending organization members.[21]

Other Legally Prohibited Conduct

Willful Failure to Discharge Board Member Duties

If a social services board member willfully neglects or refuses to discharge the duties of the office to which the board member was elected or appointed, the board member can be charged with a Class 1 misdemeanor as a criminal offense.[22] Under some circumstances, the court may remove the board member from public office as part of the sentence for the offense.

Improper Influence Regarding Hiring and Promotion of DSS Employees

As described earlier in this chapter, a social services board member is legally prohibited from influencing or attempting to influence the social services director to hire or promote the board member's spouse.[23] It is also unethical for a county social services board member to attempt to influence the social services director to hire, promote, or provide preferential treatment to *any* family member or friend of the board member.[24]

State law does not prohibit the county social services director from hiring a qualified applicant merely because the person is related to a county social services board member. Likewise, an individual is not prohibited from serving on the social services board merely because a spouse or other relative is employed by the county social services department. Being related to a county DSS employee or applicant for employment, in itself, does not create an ethical conflict for a board member. Rather, ethical conflicts are created when board members use their positions on the board to influence or coerce the director to make certain decisions around hiring or promotions.

Board members should also be aware that under State Human Resources Commission rules, the county DSS director is prohibited from hiring members of the director's immediate family (spouse, parents, siblings, children, grandparents, or grandchildren) to be employed by the county DSS.[25]

Improper Use or Disclosure of Confidential Information

As described in Chapter 9, state law allows social services board members to examine certain records of persons who have applied for or are receiving public assistance or social services from the county social services department.[26] It is unethical and illegal for a county social services board member to use or disclose any information regarding persons who have applied for or are receiving public assistance or social services for any purpose other than discharging the board's responsibilities with respect to administering public assistance and social services programs.[27] Improper use or disclosure of confidential information may violate both state and federal law.

Likewise, state law requires county employee personnel information to be kept confidential, including information regarding job applicants.[28] This means that, except in performance of their board duties, social services board members should not use or disclose information about a county DSS director's application, selection, performance, promotions, demotions, transfers, suspension, other disciplinary actions, evaluations, leave, compensation, or dismissal.[29] Only certain pieces of information from the director's personnel file are a matter of public record, as described in Chapters 8 and 14. A public official or employee who knowingly, willfully, and with malice permits any person to have access to personnel file information in violation of G.S. 153A-98 is guilty of a Class 3 misdemeanor.[30]

Another state statute, G.S. 14-234.1, prohibits board members from using nonpublic information that they learn through board service for purposes of financially benefiting themselves or others. Specifically, this statute makes it a Class 1 misdemeanor for a board member to acquire a pecuniary interest or gain a pecuniary benefit (or intentionally aid someone else in doing so) if the board member is

1. acting in anticipation of the board member's official action as a board member or by the county DSS, and the pecuniary interest or benefit may be affected by this official action; or
2. relying on nonpublic information that the board member obtained in the member's official capacity, and the pecuniary interest or benefit may be affected by that nonpublic information.

Prohibited Participation in Social Services Programs

As described in Chapter 5, there are a couple of unique conflicts of interest related to public assistance and social services that may limit an individual's ability to serve on the social services board. If one of these conflicts arises after an individual has already been appointed to the board, and the board member refuses to resign or take action to resolve the conflict, it could serve as grounds for removal of the board member.

State law expressly prohibits a county social services board member or the board member's spouse from receiving payments under the State-County Special Assistance or Medicaid programs on behalf of persons who are residents or patients in adult care or nursing homes that are owned or operated, in whole or in part, by the board member or the board member's spouse.[31]

County social services board members are prohibited from (1) being licensed as foster parents through the social services department of the county in which they serve on the social services board or (2) being supervised or considered as a placement resource by the social services department of the county in which they serve on the social services board.[32]

Outside of these specific conflicts, receiving public assistance or social services from the county social services department does not prohibit an individual from serving on the county social services board. However, board members should abstain from being involved in board discussions, investigations, or hearings about a public assistance or social services case involving the board member or a relative of the board member.

Holding Too Many Public Offices

Under North Carolina law, an individual is prohibited from holding more than

- two appointive public offices at the same time or
- one elective public office and one appointive public office at the same time.[33]

Serving on an appointed county board of social services (or an appointed consolidated human services board) is an appointive office. But a county commissioner appointed to a social services board or a consolidated human services board by the board of county commissioners (an *ex officio* appointment) is deemed to be only holding one elective public office (the office of county commissioner)—not an elected and an appointive public office.[34] In other words, service on a county social services board or consolidated human services board does not count toward the office-holding limit for that commissioner. Ex officio appointments of county commissioners are discussed in more detail in Chapter 11.

Holding Incompatible Offices

In addition to the prohibition on multiple office-holding described above, there is some older North Carolina case law recognizing a common law doctrine that prohibits incompatible office-holding.[35] This doctrine generally defines offices as "incompatible" when there is a conflict between the functions or duties of the two offices.[36] For example, this would prohibit an individual from holding two offices where one of the offices acts as a supervisor for another (i.e., a superior/subordinate relationship).

For social services boards, this means that a board member should never serve as acting or interim director of the county DSS, since the board has authority to make decisions about the director's employment (including evaluating, disciplining, and dismissing the director).

Improper Conduct of Board Members Who Are Lawyers

Social services board members who are licensed to practice law in North Carolina must comply with the Rules of Professional Conduct (Rules) adopted by the North Carolina State Bar.[37] The Rules prohibit a lawyer who has been appointed to a county social services board from considering any matter, participating in any decision, or attempting to influence any issue as a board member in which the lawyer or the lawyer's firm has any direct or indirect interest.[38]

The Rules do not prohibit a lawyer from serving on the social services board merely because the lawyer's partner, associate, or firm represents the social services board or the county department of social services, so long as the lawyer who serves on the board refrains from participating in any deliberations or actions related to the firm's legal representation of the board or department and does not attempt to influence the board's, department's, or county's actions with respect to the firm.[39]

The Rules also prohibit an attorney who serves on the social services board from directly participating in a lawsuit or other matter in which the attorney's firm is adverse to the county DSS, the board, or the DSS director.[40] The attorney's law firm must screen the attorney out from participating in the matter, the social services board must screen the attorney out from participating in the board's discussions or voting on the matter, and the attorney must make certain disclosures to the board about the attorney's relationship to the matter.[41] The attorney board member must also refrain from any expression of opinion, public or private, or any formal or informal consideration of the matter, including any communication with other board members or the county DSS director about the matter. The attorney's *law firm* is not prohibited from representing a client in such a matter, so long as these requirements are met. However, if the attorney board member is a necessary *party* to the litigation or other adverse action (in either an individual or official capacity), the attorney's firm or partner is disqualified from representing *any* party in the action.[42]

Certain Ethics Laws Applicable to the DSS Director

Remember, social services board members are public officials, not government employees. This means that they are not subject to some of the ethics laws that apply to county employees, such as the Hatch Act (Title 5 of the U.S. Code, Chapter 15) and G.S. 153A-99. However, board members should be familiar with these ethics laws, since they do apply to the county DSS director:

The Hatch Act[43] is a federal law that prohibits a state or local government employee from running for partisan political office if the employee works in a position that has duties in connection with programs financed in whole or in part by federal funds.[44]

G.S. 153A-99 prohibits county employees from (1) using their official authority or influence for the purpose of interfering with or affecting the result of an election or nomination for political office; or (2) coercing, soliciting, or compelling contributions for political or partisan purposes by another employee while on duty or in the workplace. This law also prohibits county employees from requiring other county employees to contribute funds for political or partisan purposes.

Adopting a Code of Ethics

What if a board member's conduct is unethical but does not violate the law? This presents a challenging situation for appointed social services board members, who have no general authority to discipline one another.[45] The board could ask the member to resign or to cease the unethical conduct, but the board member might refuse to do either one. To anticipate such situations, an appointed social services board may want to consider adopting its own code of ethics, along with rules of procedure that allow for the removal of a board member who violates the board's code of ethics (see Chapter 13 regarding rules of procedure and Chapter 5 regarding removal of board members).

Rules of procedure adopted by an appointed social services board regarding removal of a board member would only apply to the removal of the fifth (or third) member appointed by the majority of the board members themselves. Codes of ethics or rules of procedure adopted by appointed social services boards have no authority to bind the Social Services Commission or the board of county commissioners with respect to their decisions to remove (or not remove) board members that they appointed. Social services board members could, however, present information about a fellow board member's unethical conduct to the entity that appointed the board member (the Social Services Commission or the board of county commissioners) and ask that the appointing entity consider removing the board member.

More information on the purposes and limitations of ethical codes is available in Chapter 3 of *Ethics, Conflicts, and Offices: A Guide for Local Officials*, by A. Fleming Bell.[46]

Other Laws Applicable to County Commissioners

When the board of county commissioners serves directly as the governing board for social services in a county, the county commissioners may be subject to additional ethics and conflicts of interest requirements (that would not normally apply to appointed social services boards) due to their roles as commissioners. For example, G.S. 153A-44 imposes a duty upon each county commissioner to vote on any matter before the board of county commissioners unless the matter involves certain actual (not merely apparent) conflicts of interest for the commissioner as defined by statute. Appointed social services board members do not have a similar statutory "duty to vote."

A board of county commissioners exercising the powers and duties of a social services board also should be mindful of G.S. 14-234.3, which prohibits a county commissioner who serves as a director, officer, or governing-board member of a nonprofit organization from participating in making or administering any contracts between that nonprofit and the county.[47] Specifically, commissioners who are directors, officers, or governing-board members of a nonprofit must recuse themselves from any deliberation or vote by the board of county commissioners on a contract (including an award of money) with that nonprofit, and the recusal must be recorded with the board's clerk.[48] A knowing violation of G.S. 14-234.3 is a Class 1 misdemeanor.[49]

For more information on compliance with G.S. 14-234.3, please see *Conflicts of Interest for Public Officials on Nonprofit Boards: An Analysis of North Carolina G.S. 14-234.3*, by Kristina Wilson.[50]

Notes

1. For a more in-depth discussion of ethics for public officials (and other definitions of the term *ethics*), please see A. FLEMING BELL, II, ETHICS, CONFLICTS, AND OFFICES: A GUIDE FOR LOCAL OFFICIALS (UNC School of Government, 2d ed. 2011).
2. Conflicts of interest are discussed in more detail in Chapter 4 and Chapter 5 of BELL, *supra* note 1.
3. When the board of county commissioners is acting as the governing board for social services, the county commissioners have a duty to vote unless there is an actual conflict of interest as defined under Chapter 153A, Section 44 of the North Carolina General Statutes (hereinafter G.S.). Members of appointed boards of social services do not have a similar statutory duty to vote.
4. G.S. 14-234(a)(1).
5. G.S. 14-234(a)(2).
6. G.S. 14-234(a)(3) (emphasis added).
7. G.S. 14-234(e).
8. G.S. 14-234(f). This statute provides certain exceptions under which the void contract may continue in effect until an alternative can be arranged.
9. G.S. 14-234(a1)(4).
10. G.S. 14-234(a1)(3).
11. G.S. 14-234(a1)(2).
12. North Carolina law does not expressly authorize county social services directors to enter into contracts on behalf of the county social services department. However, a county social services director may enter into or execute a contract on behalf of the county if authorized to do so under a county ordinance or policy or pursuant to a specific state rule.
13. G.S. 14-234(b) lists additional exceptions for other types of contracts that are not described in this chapter.
14. G.S. 14-234(b)(3), (b1).
15. G.S. 14-234(b)(4), (b1).
16. G.S. 14-234(d1). Population size is determined according to the most recent official federal census.
17. G.S. 14-234(d1).
18. G.S. 133-32(a).
19. *Id.*
20. G.S. 133-32(d).
21. *Id.*
22. G.S. 14-230(a).
23. G.S. 14-234(a)(2).
24. If the board member solicits or receives a gift, favor, reward, service, or promise of reward (including a promise of future employment) in exchange for this influence, it may be a violation of G.S. 14-234(a)(3).
25. *See* Title 25, Chapter 01I, Section .1702 of the North Carolina Administrative Code (hereinafter N.C.A.C.). Specifically, the rule states, "Members of an immediate family shall not be employed within the same agency if the employment results in one member supervising another member of the employee's immediate family, or if one member will occupy a position that has influence over another member's employment, promotion, salary administration, or other related management or personnel considerations." The

DSS director occupies a position that has influence over the terms and conditions of all DSS employees' employment.

26. G.S. 108A-11.
27. G.S. 108A, §§ 11, 80.
28. G.S. 153A-98; *see also* Elkin Trib., Inc. v. Yadkin Cnty. Bd. of Cnty. Comm'rs, 331 N.C. 735 (1992).
29. G.S. 153A-98(a).
30. G.S. 153A-98(e).
31. G.S. 108A, §§ 47, 55(d).
32. 10A N.C.A.C. 70E, § .1105.
33. N.C. Const. art. VI, § 9; G.S. 128-1.1. North Carolina's law limiting multiple office-holding is discussed in detail in A. Fleming Bell, II, *Multiple Office-Holding, in* Ethics, Conflicts, and Offices: A Guide for Local Officials, *supra* note 1, ch. 6.
34. G.S. 128-1.2.
35. For a comprehensive discussion of the common law doctrine of incompatible office-holding, including applicable case law, please see A Fleming Bell, II, *Incompatible Office-Holding, in* Ethics, Conflicts, and Offices: A Guide for Local Officials, *supra* note 1, ch. 7.
36. *See* Bell, *supra* note 1, at 148.
37. The full text of the Rules is available on the North Carolina State Bar's website at https://www.ncbar.gov/for-lawyers/ethics/rules-of-professional-conduct/.
38. N.C. State Bar, Ethics Opinion CPR 290 (Oct. 14, 1981) (overruled in part by N.C. State Bar, Employment of Board Member's Law Firm, Ethics Opinion RPC 130 (Oct. 23, 1992)).
39. N.C. State Bar, Employment of Board Member's Law Firm, *supra* note 38.
40. N.C. State Bar, Implications of Service on a Public Body or Non-Profit Board, 2002 Formal Ethics Op. 2 (July 9, 2002).
41. *Id.*
42. *Id.*
43. 5 U.S.C. §§ 1501–08.
44. *See* Diane Juffras, *What Is the Hatch Act?*, UNC Sch. of Gov't, https://www.sog.unc.edu/resources/faqs/what-hatch-act (last visited Apr. 4, 2023).
45. *See* Bell, *supra* note 1, at 43–44.
46. *Id.* at 33–46.
47. G.S. 14-234.3(a).
48. *Id.* The same exceptions that apply to G.S. 14-234 also apply to this recusal requirement regarding contracts with nonprofits (*see* G.S. 14-234.3(b)), meaning G.S. 14-234.3 does not require a commissioner's recusal from involvement with a contract with a nonprofit if it falls within one of those exceptions. However, the requirements for complying with those exceptions, discussed earlier in this chapter, will generally also mandate the conflicted public official's recusal from involvement with the contract.
49. G.S. 14-234.3(b).
50. Kristina Wilson, *Conflicts of Interest for Public Officials on Nonprofit Boards: An Analysis of North Carolina G.S. 14-234.3*, Loc. Gov't L. Bull. No. 142 (UNC School of Government, Nov. 2022), https://www.sog.unc.edu/sites/default/files/reports/2022-11-21%20 20220220%20LGLB%20142.pdf.

Chapter 13

Social Services Board Meetings and Procedures

To exercise the social services board's powers and duties, board members must act together as a public body in an official meeting. North Carolina's open meetings law (Chapter 143, Article 33C of the General Statutes, hereinafter *G.S.*) establishes multiple requirements for how these meetings must be conducted, which are discussed in this chapter. Outside of the open meetings law, state law also contains requirements for social services boards regarding the frequency of board meetings, the role of the board chair, and the board's voting process. This chapter discusses these legal requirements, along with other procedural matters.

Board Secretary

In a county with an appointed county board of social services, state law designates the DSS director as the board's secretary (but allows the director to delegate this responsibility to a member of the director's staff if needed).[1] In a county with an appointed consolidated human services (CHS) board, the CHS director acts as secretary to the board.[2]

The remainder of this chapter will refer to the county DSS director as the secretary for the board, but keep in mind that this responsibility lies with the CHS director in a county with an appointed CHS board.

Board Meeting Procedures

Frequency of Board Meetings

State law requires each appointed county DSS board to meet at least once each month.[3] However, in some cases, the board may need to meet more frequently to accomplish all of its work. The board chair has authority to call additional board meetings, if needed.[4]

By contrast, consolidated human services boards are only required to meet on a quarterly basis.[5] Additional meetings of a CHS board may be called by the board chair or by three board members.[6]

Date and Time of Board Meetings

Social services boards may vote to determine the dates and times of their regular board meetings.[7] Most social services boards establish a consistent day and time for board meetings. Some boards find it more convenient to meet during the workday, while others choose to meet in the evenings to accommodate the work schedules of board members. When deciding on a schedule for regular meetings, the board should attempt to choose a time slot and day of the week that is mutually convenient for board members and the social services director.

Election and Role of the Board Chair

State law requires each board of social services to annually elect a member to serve as board chair.[8] This election must occur each year at the board's July meeting and must not be conducted in closed session.[9] Unless the board's procedures or policies provide otherwise, the board chair should be elected by a majority vote of the board members who are currently serving on the board and are present at the meeting.[10]

Each board chair serves for a term of one year and continues to serve in that role until a new chair is elected by the board.[11] Though the board chair must be elected each year, the same social services board member could be reelected for additional consecutive one-year terms as chair.

A social services board may vote to designate another board member as vice-chair, though the board is not required to do so. The board may authorize this individual to exercise the board chair's powers and duties in the event of the chair's absence, death, resignation, or removal from office.

What are the social services board chair's powers and duties?

- The chair is authorized to call additional meetings of the board, outside of the regular monthly meeting schedule.[12]
- The chair is responsible for appointing a board member to the local community child-protection team.[13]
- The chair has the implied authority and responsibility to preside at board meetings; to ensure that board meetings are conducted fairly and in accordance with the board's rules of procedure; to recognize members who wish to speak at board meetings; and to rule on motions and questions of procedure at board meetings.[14]

Other responsibilities of the social services board chair vary from county to county and person to person. In some counties, for example, the board chair functions as the board's primary spokesperson in the community or acts as a liaison between the social services board and other public bodies. In other counties, the board chair presides over meetings but does not act as an external spokesperson or liaison. Social services board members should discuss and agree upon their expectations with respect to the chair's role and responsibilities.

Board Meeting Agendas

Preparing and following an agenda for each social services board meeting can help the board be efficient and effective.

The board has discretion to develop its own procedures and practices regarding the preparation and circulation of agendas. Generally, the board chair will prepare a proposed agenda for each board meeting with input from the social services director and other board members. The social services director, acting as the board's secretary, will typically send a copy of the agenda and any additional information related to agenda items to board members at least several days before the meeting. As its first order of business at the meeting, the board decides whether items should be added to or removed from the proposed agenda, makes any additional changes to the proposed agenda, and adopts the agenda for the meeting.[15]

Some social services boards allow the director of social services to determine the agenda for every board meeting. In some cases, allowing the director to establish meeting agendas can cause board members to become passive regarding their work. The board should seek input from the director regarding the agenda but does not have to allow the director to have sole control over agenda-setting.

A social services board should ensure that adequate time is allotted for every item on the meeting agenda. The board's rules of procedure should address the length of board meetings and what the board will do if there is insufficient time to consider all the items on its agenda.

The board must provide a copy of the meeting agenda to meeting attendees if the board discusses or acts on matters by reference to a number, letter, or other designation of the matter on the board's agenda and attendees would need a copy of the agenda to understand what the board is referring to.[16]

The agendas for social services board meetings (and all records submitted to the board in connection with social services board meetings) are public records, meaning they must be made available to members of the public upon request except to the extent that they contain information that is confidential or privileged under state or federal laws. Disclosure of public records is discussed in Chapter 14 of this book.

Quorum

A *quorum* is the minimum number of board members that must be present before the board can take any official action or transact public business. If board members act at a meeting at which a quorum is not present, their actions are invalid unless they are subsequently ratified by majority vote of the board at a meeting at which a quorum is present.

State law does not specify the number of board members required to constitute a quorum of an appointed county social services board. Consequently, county social services boards should adopt local rules of procedure that specify the number of board members that will constitute a quorum.[17] In the absence of local rules, the board should consider a quorum to be a majority of the board's members (at least two members of a three-member board or at least three members of a five-member board). The social services director is not a member of the board, so the director does not count when determining whether a quorum is present.

What about other types of social services boards? For a CHS board, state law defines a quorum as a majority of the board's members.[18] For a BOCC that acts as the governing board for social services, a majority of the membership (without regard to vacancies) constitutes a quorum.[19]

Voting

Except as otherwise provided by state law or by a board's rules of procedure, all decisions by a social services board should be made by majority vote of the members who are present and constitute a quorum at an official board meeting. A board member who presides at a meeting as the board's chair or vice-chair retains the right to vote with respect to all issues coming before the board.[20] The social services director may not vote on any matter before the board, since the director is not a board member.

The state's open meetings law prohibits social services board members from voting by secret ballot.[21] Board members are allowed to vote by written ballot only if each ballot is signed by the member who voted with it and the minutes of the meeting show how each member voted.[22] The written ballots also must be retained and made available for public inspection in the office of the social services director (as the board's secretary) until the minutes of that meeting are approved.[23]

For more information on conflicts of interest that might require board members to recuse themselves from voting, please see Chapter 12 of this book.

Rules of Procedure

Aside from the open meetings law, state law provides little guidance as to procedures for social services board meetings. Accordingly, social services boards have discretion to establish their own local rules of procedure, so long as those rules do not contradict requirements established by state or federal law. At a minimum, each social services board should consider adopting rules of procedure regarding

- scheduling board meetings;
- determining and circulating the agendas for board meetings;

- conducting business at board meetings, including quorum requirements;
- appointment and removal of the third or fifth member of the social services board;
- electing the board chair;
- remote participation in meetings;
- evaluating the board's work; and
- evaluating the director's performance.

The UNC School of Government has developed model rules of procedure for local appointed boards that social services boards can use as a starting point for adopting their own rules of procedure. For more information, please read *Suggested Procedural Rules for Local Appointed Boards*, by Trey Allen and A. Fleming Bell.[24] These suggested rules incorporate the requirements of the state's open meetings law and include model rules regarding board meetings, adoption of meeting agendas, order of business, the duties of the board chair, quorum, minutes, public hearings, appointments, committees, motions, debate, and voting.

Complying with the Open Meetings Law

A social services board is a "public body" for purposes of North Carolina's open meetings law.[25] North Carolina's open meetings law focuses on two main requirements that promote transparency about the meetings of public bodies. First, the public must have *notice* of official meetings of public bodies, and second, the public must have *access* to such meetings. Additionally, the open meetings law requires each public body to keep full and accurate minutes of its official meetings. These requirements, described in more detail in the remaining sections of this chapter, are intended to ensure that members of the public are better informed about how public bodies are carrying out their official responsibilities. As a helpful reference for questions about the open meetings law's requirements, please read *Open Meetings and Local Governments in North Carolina: Some Questions and Answers*, by Frayda Bluestein and David Lawrence.[26]

The open meetings law's requirements regarding public notice and public access are triggered whenever a majority of the board's members meet, assemble, or gather together—in person or via simultaneous electronic or telephonic communication—for the purpose of conducting a hearing, participating in deliberations, voting, or otherwise transacting "public business."[27] This means that board members must be careful to discuss and deliberate on matters of public business related to their board duties only in the context of an official meeting that meets the notice and access requirements of the open meetings law. Even group telephone calls, web conferences, and simultaneous online chat or email threads involving the majority of the board's members have the potential to trigger the requirements of the open meetings law.

Board members can still engage in social gatherings without providing public notice or access, so long as they are not engaging in public business during the

Table 13.1. Types of Board Meetings

Regular meeting	A meeting held on a regular date and at a regular time and place specified in a schedule filed with the clerk of the board of county commissioners.
Special meeting	Any meeting (other than an emergency or recessed meeting) that is held at a date, time, or place other than the regular date, time, or place specified in the schedule of regular board meetings on file with the clerk.
Emergency meeting	A meeting called because of generally unexpected circumstances that require immediate consideration by the board. Only business connected with the emergency may be considered at an emergency meeting.
Recessed meeting	A continuation (reconvening) of an earlier regular, special, or emergency meeting.

Note: See G.S. 143-318.12.

gathering and the gathering is not called or held to evade the spirit and purposes of the open meetings law.[28] For example, three members from a five-person social services board could have a dinner party together without triggering the open meetings law's requirements but might violate the open meetings law if they use that dinner party as an opportunity to discuss the potential termination of the county's DSS director.

Public Notice of Board Meetings

North Carolina's open meetings law requires a social services board to give public notice of all of its official meetings (including those at which all of the board's business will be conducted in closed session) as well as the official meetings of committees or subcommittees of the board.[29] This means that the board may never hold a secret meeting (one without advance notice to the public), even when the entire meeting will be conducted in closed session.

The type of public notice that must be given for social services board meetings depends on whether the meeting is a regular meeting, a special meeting, an emergency meeting, or a recessed meeting. Table 13.1 defines each type of meeting. Each type of meeting has its own notice requirements set forth in the open meetings law.

Notice of Regular Meetings

If a social services board establishes a regular date, time, and place for its meetings, the board must file a regular meeting schedule with the clerk of the county's board of commissioners.[30] The social services board must also post its regular meeting schedule on either the county's website or the county DSS's website.[31] Once the board's regular meeting schedule is filed with the clerk and posted online, the board does not have to give any additional public notice of any board meeting held at the regular date, time, and location established in the schedule.

If the board wants to change its regular meeting date, time, or location, the social services director or the board chair must file the board's revised regular meeting schedule with the clerk of the county's BOCC at least seven calendar days before the next regular board meeting that will be held under the revised schedule.[32] The revised schedule must also be posted on either the county's website or the county DSS's website.[33]

Notice of Special Meetings

Whenever a social services board holds a special meeting, the board must provide notice at least forty-eight hours before the time of the meeting, notifying the public of the date, time, place, and *purpose* of the meeting by

1. posting the notice on the principal bulletin board of the county DSS or at the door of the board's usual meeting room;[34]
2. mailing, emailing, or delivering the notice to each person, newspaper, wire service, radio station, and television station that has filed a written request for such notices with the clerk or secretary of the board (often called a "sunshine list");[35] and
3. posting the notice on either the county's website or the county DSS's website.[36]

If the county DSS or the building containing the usual meeting room is closed to the public continuously for forty-eight hours before the time of the special meeting, the notice that is normally posted on the bulletin board or meeting room door must instead be posted on the door of the building (or on the building in an area accessible to the public).[37] If the BOCC is acting as the social services board, the commissioners can only discuss subjects in the special meeting that were listed on the notice of the meeting.[38]

Notice of Emergency Meetings

The board must give notice of an emergency meeting immediately after board members have been notified of the meeting.[39] The notice must be given to any local newspaper, wire service, radio station, or television station that has filed a written request for such notices with the clerk or secretary of the board. The board may give notice of an emergency meeting by email, by telephone, or by the same method used to notify the members of the board.

Notice of Recessed Meetings

To continue a meeting at a later time or date, a motion to recess the meeting must be approved by a majority vote of the board. The time and place at which the regular, special, or emergency meeting is to be continued (reconvened) must be announced in open session during the meeting.[40] The time and place of the recessed meeting should also be posted on either the county's website or the county DSS's website.[41]

Public Access to Board Meetings

Social services boards may choose the location of their regular monthly board meetings. However, the board must consider public accessibility when choosing a location, because the open meetings law requires a public body to take reasonable measures to provide for public access to its official meetings.[42] Among other things, this means the social services board should take reasonable measures to ensure adequate seating for the number of people that typically attend the board's meetings (though the board does not have to provide overflow seating or ensure space for a larger-than-usual crowd).[43] For example, holding a board meeting in a room that is only large enough to provide seating for the board's members may violate the open meetings law if larger rooms are readily available, since using the smaller room would completely exclude members of the public from attending.[44]

The board should also attempt to choose a meeting location that is reasonably accessible to individuals with disabilities and to individuals who must rely on public transportation.[45]

If the BOCC is acting as the social services board, it is generally required to hold all its meetings within the county except in certain circumstances set forth in G.S. 153A-40(c).

Public Comment and Recording at Board Meetings

The open meetings law gives any person the right to attend open sessions of official meetings of a social services board.[46] However, the open meetings law does not give members of the public a right to address the social services board during the board meeting or participate in the board's discussions. A social services board may choose to include a public comment period in its meetings but is not required by law to do so.

The board chair may direct any person, including a board member, to leave a board meeting if the person is willfully interrupting, disrupting, or disturbing the meeting.[47] Willfully refusing to leave the meeting after such an order constitutes a Class 2 misdemeanor.[48]

The open meetings law allows any person to photograph, film, tape-record, or otherwise reproduce any part of an open meeting of the social services board.[49] Any radio or television station may also broadcast all or part of an open board meeting. The board may regulate the placement and use of recording or broadcasting equipment if necessary to prevent undue interference with its meetings.[50]

Closed Sessions in Board Meetings

Every official meeting of the social services board must be open to the public.[51] However, sometimes the board needs to hold part of the meeting in "closed session," meaning members of the public are excluded when the board is discussing certain matters. Closed sessions must occur within the context of an official meeting—a meeting that the public has received notice of in accordance with the open meetings law.[52] This means that the social services board cannot hold a secret meeting (one without notice to the public) even if the board intends to conduct all of its business in closed session.

When a social services board holds a closed session, only the board's members have a right to attend. The board may allow the social services director, social services staff, or others to attend a closed session if the board chooses to do so and their participation will be helpful to the board. However, the board should have a logical justification for who it permits to join a closed session instead of making arbitrary decisions about which members of the public (non-board members) are allowed to attend.[53]

Procedure for Going into Closed Session

Even if most or all of the board's business will be conducted in a closed session, the board must start the meeting in open session. In order to go into closed session, a board member must make a motion (in open session) to go into closed session, and that motion must be adopted by a majority of the board members present and voting.[54]

The motion must state the purpose of the closed session, which must be one (or more) of the permissible purposes listed in G.S. 143-318.11(a).[55] If the purpose is to prevent the disclosure of privileged or confidential information, the motion must state the name or citation of the law that makes the information privileged or confidential. If the purpose is to consult with an attorney and preserve attorney-client privilege, the motion must identify the parties in each existing lawsuit about which the board expects to receive advice during the closed session.

During a closed session, the board may not discuss or take action on any matter outside of the purpose(s) specified in the motion to meet in closed session (or outside of the permitted purposes described in G.S. 143-318.11(a)). If the board wants to discuss a different matter in closed session, other than what was specified in the motion, it must reconvene in open session and adopt another motion to meet in closed session for a different permitted purpose.

Permitted Purposes for Closed Sessions

A social services board is not allowed to go into closed session for any reason or to discuss any topic. Instead, the open meetings law provides only a limited list of allowable purposes for going into closed session. This means that a social services board may meet in closed session only

- to prevent the disclosure of information that is privileged or confidential under state or federal law or is not considered to be a public record under North Carolina's public records law;[56]
- to consult with an attorney employed or retained by the social services board in order to preserve the attorney-client privilege (but not to discuss general policy matters);[57]

- to consider the qualifications, competence, performance, character, fitness, conditions of appointment, or conditions of initial employment of the county social services director;[58]
- to hear or investigate a complaint, charge, or grievance by or against the county director of social services or another social services employee;[59]
- to plan, conduct, or hear reports concerning investigations of alleged criminal misconduct;[60] or
- to consider or take action with respect to other matters listed in G.S. 143-318.11(a).

Prohibited Purposes for Closed Sessions

The social services board cannot meet in closed session for any purpose other than those listed in the open meetings law at G.S. 143-318.11(a). The open meetings law also explicitly prohibits the board from meeting in closed session for the following purposes.

1. While the board may discuss a *specific* public employee or official (such as the DSS director) in closed session, the board may not discuss issues related to general DSS personnel policies in closed session.[61]
2. The board may not take final action to appoint or dismiss the county social services director in closed session.[62] However, the board may reach a tentative consensus on such a decision during a closed session and then take the final action to appoint or dismiss the director in open session.[63]
3. The board may not use a closed session to consider the qualifications, competence, performance, character, fitness, appointment, or removal of a member of the social services board, or to discuss or evaluate the board's own performance.[64]

Keeping Minutes of Board Meetings

The open meetings law requires each social services board to keep full and accurate minutes of its official meetings, including closed sessions.[65] Minutes of social services board meetings are typically recorded in written form, but the board may choose to keep minutes in the form of audio or video recordings.[66] The primary purpose of these minutes is to provide evidence that the board's actions followed proper procedure.[67]

The county social services director, as the board's secretary, should take minutes of social services board meetings (or delegate this duty to a social services employee if the director is unavailable).[68] If the director or the employee who has been designated to take minutes is excluded from a closed session of a board meeting, minutes of the closed session should be taken by a board member (or another person designated by the board who is in the closed session).

For more information about requirements related to keeping minutes, including a more in-depth discussion of some of the topics mentioned in this section, please see *"Full and Accurate" Minutes: A Primer,* by Trey Allen.[69]

Contents of the Minutes

The board's minutes must accurately reflect the substance of all official actions taken by the board and the vote by which action was taken. The board is not required to summarize or quote each member's comments with respect to an issue or to record the names of the members who voted for or against a motion (unless the board voted by written ballot).[70] If the board doesn't take any official action at a meeting, the minutes only need to document that a meeting occurred.[71] However, a board may want to include additional detail in the minutes beyond what is legally required, since the minutes also serve as a historical record of the board's work.[72]

General Accounts of Closed Sessions

If a social services board meets in closed session, the board must (in addition to recording minutes) prepare a "general account of the closed session so that a person not in attendance would have a reasonable understanding of what transpired."[73] The general account of a closed session may consist of a written narrative or an audio or audiovisual recording of the session.

Approving Meeting Minutes

Though not required by the open meetings law, it is important for social services boards to officially approve the minutes of their meetings. Among other things, this gives board members the opportunity to correct errors in the record. If the board determines that the proposed minutes are incorrect or incomplete, the board may vote to amend the minutes. The motion to approve minutes from a prior meeting should occur in open session, unless the discussion about the minutes or general account of a closed session would "frustrate the purpose" of the closed session (for example, by revealing confidential information).[74] In such a case, the board could approve the minutes or general account of the closed session in a subsequent closed session.[75]

Meeting Minutes Are Public Records

The minutes (and proposed or draft minutes) of social services board meetings are public records, meaning they must be made available to a member of the public upon request under the state's public records law except to the extent that they contain information that is privileged or confidential under state or federal law.[76] General accounts and minutes of closed sessions are also public records, but can be withheld from public inspection for "so long as public inspection would frustrate the purpose of a closed session."[77]

The social services board and director must preserve the minutes of board meetings—along with meeting agendas and copies of supporting documentation submitted and discussed during meetings—until they are authorized to be destroyed pursuant to a records retention and disposition schedule established by the state Department of Natural and Cultural Resources.[78] The official minutes of board meetings, as well as all attachments necessary to understand the board's actions during a board meeting, must be retained permanently.[79] For more information on records retention and disposition requirements, please see Chapter 14 of this book.

Remote Meetings and Remote Participation

Appointed county DSS boards and CHS boards may wish to hold some meetings remotely via teleconference, videoconference, or other electronic means. Before undertaking a remote meeting or allowing a board member to participate in a meeting remotely, a social services board should adopt rules of procedure regarding remote meetings.

The board's rules of procedure should address key questions such as:

- Do remote participants count toward quorum for purposes of conducting board business?[80]
- Are remote participants entitled to vote?[81]
- Who has authority to decide whether a meeting will be held remotely? Can the board chair make this determination unilaterally?
- What types of remote participation are allowed? For example, would teleconferencing be sufficient, or does a board member need to be visible by video as well?
- Is a single member of the board allowed to participate in a meeting remotely? Or is remote participation only permitted if the entire board meeting is held remotely?
- Is there any limit to the number of times an individual board member may participate remotely in a given year?

Special Requirements for Remote Meetings

If the board holds a meeting using teleconference or other electronic means, the open meetings law requires the board to provide "a location and means whereby members of the public may listen to the meeting."[82] The board must specify that location information in the notice of the board meeting. At a minimum, this means the board must provide an online meeting link or teleconference information to the public in advance of the meeting. It also means, however, that the board must provide a physical location where members of the public may listen to the meeting (for example, for an individual who wants to attend but does not have internet or phone access at home).[83]

The open meetings law does not require the board to provide any way for members of the public to speak to or communicate with the board during a remote meeting. In other words, members of the public must be able to *hear* the board meeting, but the board does not have to provide a method for the public to *contribute* to the board meeting. However, a board may want to provide a way for members of the public to speak during remote meetings if the board has decided (in its own rules of procedure) to allow public comment periods during its meetings.

Other Suggested Rules

If a social services board wishes to authorize remote meetings or individual remote participation in meetings, it should also consider adopting the following rules to promote transparency, accuracy, and efficiency.[84]

- A board member participating by simultaneous communication shall be counted as present for quorum purposes only during the period while simultaneous communication is maintained for that member.
- Any board members participating by a method of simultaneous communication in which they cannot be physically seen by the board must identify themselves
    1. when the roll is taken or the remote meeting is commenced;
    2. prior to participating in the deliberations, including making motions, proposing amendments, and raising points of order; and
    3. prior to voting.
- All documents to be considered during the remote meeting must be provided to each member of the board.
- The method of simultaneous communication must allow for any board member to (1) hear what is said by the other board members, (2) hear what is said by any individual addressing the board, and (3) be heard by the other board members when speaking to the board.
- All votes must be by roll call (no voting by secret or written ballots).
- The minutes of the remote meeting must reflect that the meeting was conducted by use of simultaneous communication, which members were participating by simultaneous communication, and when such members joined or left the remote meeting.
- All chats, instant messages, texts, or other written communications between board members regarding the transaction of the public business shall be treated as public records.[85]
- The remote meeting will be simultaneously streamed live online so that simultaneous live audio (and video, if any) of the meeting is available to the public. If the remote meeting is conducted by conference call, the board will provide the public with an opportunity to dial in or stream the audio live.

Remote Meetings During Emergency Declarations

A special set of requirements apply to remote meetings when the governor or the General Assembly has declared a state of emergency and the board is within the emergency area. Under such circumstances, the board should comply with the requirements of G.S. 166A-19.24, which establishes remote-meeting requirements applicable to public bodies during emergency declarations. If the board's own rules of procedure conflict with the requirements in G.S. 166A-19.24, the board should follow G.S. 166A-19.24.

Remote Participation and Quorum

Since appointed county boards of social services have no statutory quorum require-ments, there is no indication that physical presence at board meetings is legally required to constitute a quorum. Accordingly, a social services board can establish in its own rules of procedure whether remote participation counts towards quorum.

Regarding consolidated human services boards, G.S. 153A-77 says that "[a] major-ity of the members shall constitute a quorum," but does not use the word *present* or otherwise indicate that physical presence is required.[86] Consequently, an appointed consolidated human services board may also establish in its rules of procedure whether a remote participant counts toward constituting a quorum.

What about remote participation when the board of county commissioners is serving as the governing board for social services? The statute that defines quorum for boards of county commissioners does not specifically say that members must be physically present to count toward a quorum.[87] It does, however, use the term *present,* which could be interpreted as requiring physical presence (or alternatively, could be read to include presence via electronic or telephonic means). County com-missioners should consult with the county attorney to determine whether engaging in remote meetings is advisable.[88]

Liability for Violating the Open Meetings Law

Any person who believes that the social services board has violated the open meet-ings law may seek injunctive relief in district or superior court.[89] If a judge finds that the board violated the open meetings law, the judge may enjoin the board from threatened or continuing violations of the open meetings law or the recurrence of past violations of the law.[90]

Likewise, any individual may file a lawsuit in superior court requesting the entry of a judgment declaring that an action of the social services board was taken, consid-ered, discussed, or deliberated in violation of the open meetings law.[91] If a superior court judge makes such a finding, the judge may declare the action taken by the board in violation of the law to be null and void.[92]

If a court finds that the social services board has violated the open meetings law, the court may order the board to pay the attorney's fees of the person or entity that sued the board.[93] If the court finds that a board member knowingly or inten-tionally violated the open meetings law, the court may order the board member to *personally* pay all or part of the plaintiff's attorney's fees.[94] However, there is some protection from this potential personal liability: the court may not order a board member to pay the plaintiff's attorney's fees if the board member (or the board as a whole) sought and followed the advice of an attorney with respect to the board's actions.[95] Accordingly, if the board is confused or unclear about the open meetings law's requirements with respect to a certain decision or procedure, the board should attempt to consult with an attorney before acting, if possible.

Notes

1. G.S. 108A, § 14(a)(1) (designating the DSS director as the board's secretary), 14(b) (allowing the director to delegate responsibilities to a member of the director's staff).
2. G.S. 153A-77(e)(4).
3. G.S. 108A-7.
4. *Id.*
5. G.S. 153A-77(c).
6. *Id.*
7. If the board chair calls a special or emergency meeting, the chair may determine the date and time of that meeting. However, the chair should attempt (to the extent possible) to choose a reasonable date and time when board members are likely to be available.
8. G.S. 108A-7 (county boards of social services); *see also* G.S. 153A-77(c) (CHS boards).
9. G.S. 108A-7; *see also* G.S. 143-318.11(a)(6) (prohibiting a public body from considering the qualifications or appointment of a member during a closed session of an official meeting). The fact that a board member has been nominated to serve as chair does not disqualify the nominee from participating in the election of the board's chair.
10. This vote should include newly appointed board members if they have taken their oaths of office.
11. G.S. 108A-7.
12. *Id.*; *see also* G.S. 153A-77(c) (providing that a special meeting of a CHS board may be called by the chair or by three board members).
13. G.S. 7B-1407(b)(6).
14. Any board member may make a motion to appeal the board chair's decision regarding a procedural matter, and the board may affirm or reverse the chair's decision by majority vote.
15. The agenda may be changed during the meeting after its adoption, but only by a majority vote of the board.
16. G.S. 143-318.13(c).
17. It is customary, though not required, to define a quorum as a majority of the board's members. A social services board could require the presence of *more* than a majority of the board's membership for board action (for example, four or five members of a five-member board), but doing so might prevent the board from acting promptly.
18. G.S. 153A-77(c).
19. G.S. 153A-43.
20. The board chair or vice-chair cannot, however, cast a *second* vote as a tie-breaker.
21. *See* G.S. 143-318.13(b).
22. *See id.*
23. *See id.*
24. Trey Allen & A. Fleming Bell, II, Suggested Procedural Rules for Local Appointed Boards (UNC School of Government, 2020).
25. *See* G.S. 143-318.10(b) (defining *public body*).
26. Frayda S. Bluestein & David M. Lawrence, Open Meetings and Local Governments in North Carolina: Some Questions and Answers (UNC School of Government, 8th ed. 2017).
27. G.S. 143-318.10(d).
28. *Id.*
29. G.S. 143-318.12.

30. G.S. 143-318.12(a)(2).
31. *See* G.S. 143-318.12(d). The statute imposes this requirement "if a public body has a Web site." Some counties have a web page where notices of board meetings (including local appointed boards) are typically posted. In other counties, information about the social services board may be customarily posted to a separate website or county website subpage devoted to the county DSS. The clerk to the BOCC may be able to advise a social services board on the best location for this web-based notice.
32. *See* G.S. 143-318.12(a).
33. *Id.* See *supra* note 31 regarding this requirement.
34. G.S. 143-318.12(b)(2).
35. *Id.* The board may require each newspaper, wire service, radio station, and television station submitting a written request for notice to renew the request annually. The board may require individual persons (other than the media) to renew their requests for notice quarterly.
36. G.S. 143-318.12(e). See *supra* note 31 regarding this requirement. For special meetings, this notice requirement technically only applies if the website is maintained by an employee of the public body. However, best practice is to provide this online notice regardless of who maintains the website, since many members of the public use county websites to stay informed about meetings of their elected and appointed officials.
37. G.S. 143-318.12(b)(2).
38. G.S. 153A-40(b).
39. G.S. 143-318.12(b)(3).
40. G.S. 143-318.12(b)(1).
41. G.S. 143-318.12(e). See *supra* note 31 regarding this requirement. For recessed meetings, this notice requirement technically only applies if the website is maintained by an employee of the public body. However, best practice is to provide this online notice regardless of who maintains the website, since many members of the public use county websites to stay informed about meetings of their elected and appointed officials.
42. G.S. 143, art. 33C; Garlock v. Wake Cnty. Bd. of Educ., 211 N.C. App. 200, 223 (2011).
43. Hildebran Heritage & Dev. Ass'n v. Town of Hildebran, 252 N.C. App. 286, 294 (2017) (finding that a lack of overflow seating or external speakers, absent more, did not constitute an unreasonable failure of access under the open meetings law).
44. *See Garlock*, 211 N.C. App. at 226–27 (2011).
45. The open meetings law does not require special accommodations at public meetings for a disabled member of the public, as opposed to a nondisabled member of the public. However, other state and federal statutes that govern access to public facilities by persons with disabilities (such as the Americans with Disabilities Act, 42 U.S.C. § 12101–12213, and the Persons with Disabilities Protection Act, G.S. 168A) may impose such reasonable accommodation requirements.
46. G.S. 143-318.10(a).
47. *See* G.S. 143-318.17.
48. *Id.*
49. G.S. 143-318.14(a).
50. G.S. 143-318.14(b).
51. G.S. 143-318.10(a).
52. G.S. 143-318.11(c).
53. See Question 87 in BLUESTEIN & LAWRENCE, *supra* note 26.
54. G.S. 143-318.11(c).
55. G.S. 143-318.11(c).
56. G.S. 143-318.11(a)(1). *See also* G.S. 108A-80 (making records of persons who have applied for or received public assistance or social services from a county social services department confidential); G.S. 153-98 (making county employee personnel file information confidential).

57. G.S. 143-318.11(a)(3). The mere fact that an attorney retained or employed by a social services board participates in a board meeting does not in itself justify holding a closed session. To go into closed session, the board must be discussing a legal issue with the attorney that necessitates acting to preserve attorney-client privilege. This could include discussing potential, threatened, or active litigation, but the allowable discussion is not limited to litigation-related matters so long as some legal issue is involved. If the board has approved or considered a settlement in closed session, the terms of that settlement must be reported to the board and entered into its minutes as soon as possible within a reasonable time after the settlement is concluded.

58. G.S. 143-318.11(a)(6).

59. G.S. 143-318.11(a)(6). A social services board generally has no authority to investigate or hear complaints, charges, or grievances from social services employees unless they have been made against the DSS director. In that instance, the board may find it necessary to investigate or hear such matters in order to determine whether there is a basis for disciplining or dismissing the director.

60. G.S. 143-318.11(a)(7).

61. G.S. 143-318.11(a)(6).

62. G.S. 143-318.11(a)(6).

63. *See* Maready v. City of Winston-Salem, 342 N.C. 708, 732 (1996).

64. G.S. 143-318.11(a)(6).

65. G.S. 143-318.10(e).

66. G.S. 143-318.10(e).

67. See Question 178 in BLUESTEIN & LAWRENCE, *supra* note 26.

68. *See* G.S. 108A, § 14(a)(1) (designating the DSS director as the board's secretary), 14(b) (allowing the director to delegate responsibilities to a member of the director's staff).

69. Trey Allen, *"Full and Accurate" Minutes: A Primer,* LOC. GOV'T L. BULL. No. 140 (UNC School of Government, January 2019), https://www.sog.unc.edu/publications/bulletins/full-and-accurate-minutes-primer.

70. G.S. 143-318.13(b).

71. See Question 178 in BLUESTEIN & LAWRENCE, *supra* note 26; *see also* Maready v. City of Winston-Salem, 342 N.C. 708, 733 (1996).

72. See Question 178 in BLUESTEIN & LAWRENCE, *supra* note 26.

73. G.S. 143-318.10(e).

74. *See id.*

75. For more information about the topic of approving confidential closed-session minutes (including other options for doing so), please see Frayda Bluestein, *How to Approve Minutes and General Accounts of Closed Sessions,* COATES' CANONS: NC LOC. GOV'T L. (blog) (June 5, 2018), https://canons.sog.unc.edu/2018/06/how-to-approve-minutes-and-general-accounts-of-closed-sessions/.

76. G.S. 143-318.10(e).

77. *Id.*

78. *See* N.C. DEP'T OF NAT. & CULTURAL RES., GENERAL RECORDS SCHEDULE: LOCAL GOVERNMENT AGENCIES, items 1.47, 1.54 (Oct. 1, 2021), https://archives.ncdcr.gov/government/local (scroll to the table and select General Records Schedule: Local Government Agencies).

79. *See id.*, item 1.54.

80. Since appointed county boards of social services have no statutory quorum requirements, there is no indication that physical presence at meetings is legally required to constitute a quorum. Accordingly, a social services board can establish in its own rules of procedure whether a remote participant counts toward quorum. The statute applying to CHS boards says that "[a] majority of the members shall constitute a quorum," but it does not use the term *present* or indicate that physical presence is required.

81. Presumably, if a board member's remote participation counts for purposes of quorum, it should count for purposes of voting as well. However, it is a best practice to clarify that remote votes are valid in local rules of procedure in order to avoid a future challenge to voting results.

82. G.S. 143-318.13.

83. In light of modern technological advances, it is unclear whether the requirement to "provide a location and means whereby members of the public may listen to the meeting" is satisfied by simply providing an online link or teleconference-access information, or whether a public body is still required to provide a physical space and equipment for the public to listen to the remote meeting. A cautious approach would be to provide access to a room in a county building with a telephone, computer, or projector where members of the public could listen to the meeting.

84. These suggested rules are based on some of the requirements of G.S. 166A-19.24. That statute only applies upon issuance of a declaration of emergency under G.S. 166A-19.20, but the wording of the statute provides a helpful roadmap for appointed boards that want to adopt rules regarding remote meetings.

85. Like other records created by the board, these electronic communications may be withheld from the public if they were created during a closed session and disclosing them to the public would "frustrate the purpose" of the closed session. *See* G.S. 143-318.10.

86. *See* G.S. 153A-77(c).

87. *See* G.S. 153A-43.

88. For more information about this topic, please see Frayda S. Bluestein, *Remote Participation in Local Government Board Meetings*, Loc. Gov't L. Bull. No. 133 (UNC School of Government, Aug. 2013); also see Frayda Bluestein, *Public Meetings After the Lifting of the State-Level State of Emergency*, Coates' Canons: NC Loc. Gov't L. (blog) (July 6, 2021), https://canons.sog.unc.edu/2021/07/public-meetings-after-the-lifting-of-the-state-level-state-of-emergency/.

89. G.S. 143-318.16; G.S. 143-318.16A.

90. G.S. 143-318.16(a).

91. G.S. 143-318.16A.

92. G.S. 143-318.16A(a).

93. G.S. 143-318.16B.

94. *Id.*

95. *Id.*

Chapter 14

The Public Records Law

Members of the general public have a right to inspect or copy any record that a board member, county social services director, or county social services employee makes or receives "in the transaction of public business."[1] This broad right of access is established by North Carolina's public records law (Chapter 132 of the North Carolina General Statutes (hereinafter G.S.)). The scope of the public's right of access to records, limitations on public access to records, and records retention requirements are all discussed in this chapter.

What Is a Public Record?

Public record refers to any document, paper, letter, map, book, photograph, film, sound recording, tape recording, electronic data-processing record, email, text message, artifact, or other documentary material that is made or received in connection with the transaction of public business by any agency of North Carolina government or its subdivisions (including local social services boards and agencies).[2]

It is the content and purpose of a record—not its location—that determines whether it is subject to the public records law.[3] For example, text messages or emails sent or received by board members on their personal cell phones or through their personal email accounts may be public records if they involve the transaction of public business.

The Right to Access Public Records

Any member of the public has a right to inspect and examine public records "at reasonable times and under reasonable supervision."[4] Likewise, any member of the public has the right to obtain copies of public records, which must be furnished "as promptly as possible" following a request for such copies.[5] The public records law does not provide any hard-and-fast rule for promptness, meaning that the timeframe for responding to a request for copies likely depends on factors such as the nature of the request and the personnel capacity of the agency.[6] A public agency or board's obligation to fulfill requests for inspection or copies of public records can be satisfied by making a record available online in a format that allows someone to view it and to print it or save it.[7]

The public records law does not define "reasonable times" or "as promptly as possible," which leaves some ambiguity about how much time public officials have to respond to records requests. This will depend on factors such as the nature of the request, the availability of personnel to respond to the request, the location of the records, and whether the records must be redacted before being produced.[8]

Limitations on the Right to Access Public Records

The right to access public records is not absolute. Many state laws create exceptions to the public's right to access public records, either by making the records confidential or by exempting them from public access. The social services board must not disclose any record in response to a public records request if that record is confidential under state or federal law.

Some of the exceptions to the right of access that are most relevant to social services boards are described below.

Social Services Records

Any record regarding a person applying for or receiving social services or public assistance is confidential and may not be disclosed to the public.[9]

Closed-Session Minutes or General Accounts

Meeting minutes and general accounts recorded by the board during a closed session may be withheld from the public "so long as public inspection would frustrate the purpose of a closed session."[10]

Personnel Records

Except in limited circumstances described in G.S. 153A-98, the board may not disclose any personnel file information regarding a current or former director of social services (or any other county social services employee).[11] However, G.S. 153A-98(b) establishes a list of particular information about a county employee that *is* a matter of public record and must be disclosed upon request.

Attorney-Client Communications

The board may withhold from the public any communications by an attorney made within the scope of the attorney-client relationship concerning (1) any claim by or against the social services board, the social services department, or the county, or (2) the prosecution, defense, settlement or litigation of any judicial action or administrative proceeding to which the board is a party or by which the board may be directly affected.[12] However, these communications become public records three years from the date they are received by the board.

Sensitive Identifying Information

The board may not disclose information that can be used to access a person's financial resources, such as a person's social security number, tax identification number, driver's license or state identification card number, passport number, checking or savings account number, credit or debit card number, PIN (personal identification number), digital signature, biometric data, fingerprints, or passwords.[13]

Other exemptions exist in state law for criminal investigation information, trial preparation materials, medical records, contract bid documents, and records involving public security, among others.

What if a requested record contains some information that is confidential and other information that is public? Unless an exception prohibits the disclosure of an *entire* record, the board should redact any confidential or nonpublic information and then disclose the public (nonredacted) parts of the record in response to a records request.[14] Whenever possible, the board should consult with legal counsel before disclosing any records to ensure that the information being disclosed is public and not confidential.

Records Versus Information

It is important to remember that the public records law gives the public a right to access existing *records*, not *information*. This means that if a member of the public asks for a record that does not already exist, the board is not obligated to compile information or create a *new* record in response to the request.[15]

There is one important exception to this general rule, which relates to county personnel information. As described earlier in this chapter, G.S. 153A-98 makes most personnel file information confidential but also establishes a list of personnel information (not just records) that must be made available upon request. The following information is a matter of public record about any county employee (including the social services director) and must be provided upon request even if it is not part of an existing record:

- the employee's name;
- the employee's age;
- the date of the employee's original employment or appointment;
- the terms of any employment contract, whether written or oral;
- the employee's current position, title, and salary;
- the date and amount of each increase or decrease in the employee's salary (including pay, benefits, incentives, bonuses, and deferred and all other forms of compensation);

- the date and type of the employee's most recent promotion, demotion, transfer, suspension, separation, or other change in position classification;
- the date and general description of the reasons for each promotion;
- the date and type of each dismissal, suspension, or demotion for disciplinary reasons (if the disciplinary action was a dismissal, the written notice of the final decision setting forth the basis of the dismissal is also a matter of public record); and
- the office or station to which the employee is currently assigned.[16]

Responsibility for Responding to Public Records Requests

Who is responsible for responding to public records requests on behalf of a social services board? The public records law states that the "custodian of public records" is responsible for responding to such requests and defines the custodian as "[t]he public official in charge of an office having public records."[17] The director of social services is the records custodian for all records created or maintained by the department of social services. It is less clear who should act as the custodian of records created or maintained by an appointed social services board.[18]

In some counties, the clerk to the board of commissioners may serve (either by policy or practice) as the custodian of records created by appointed county boards. In a county where this is not the case, the social services board could designate its board chair to serve as the board's custodian of records in its rules of procedure. In either case, each social services board member is a public official and retains responsibility for preserving records that are in the board member's custody. Social services board members should work together to respond to public records requests, and they should seek counsel from the county clerk and the county attorney when they are unsure of whether a record can or should be disclosed to the public.

Liability for Denial of Access to Records

Any person who is denied access to public records or copies of public records may seek a court order compelling disclosure or copying of the records.[19] If a party successfully compels the disclosure of public records from the board, the court must allow that party to recover its reasonable attorneys' fees from the county.[20] However, the court may not assess attorneys' fees against the county if the court finds that the board acted in reasonable reliance on

- a court judgment or order applicable to the board;
- the published opinion of a North Carolina appellate court, an order of the North Carolina Business Court, or a final order of a North Carolina superior or district court; or
- a written opinion, decision, or letter of the North Carolina Attorney General.[21]

Framework for Responding to Public Records Requests

UNC School of Government professor Frayda Bluestein has created a four-step framework that social services board members may find useful for analyzing public records requests.[a]

1. **Does a record exist that corresponds to the request?**
   a. If not, no disclosure is required.
   b. If so, continue to question 2.

2. **Is the record "made or received in the transaction of public business"?**
   a. If not, no disclosure is required.
   b. If so, continue to question 3.

3. **Is there an exception in the law that applies (for example, is this a confidential record)?**
   a. If not, the requested access must be provided.
   b. If so, continue to question 4.

4. **Does the exception apply to the entire record or only to certain information? Does the exception prohibit disclosure or merely deny the right of access?**
   a. If a prohibition applies to the entire record, do not disclose. If it applies only to certain information, redact that information and then disclose.
   b. If there is no right of access to some or all of the information, but releasing the record is not prohibited, determine whether or not to release the entire record or a redacted record.

---

[a] *See* FRAYDA S. BLUESTEIN, PUBLIC RECORDS IN NORTH CAROLINA, UNC School of Government (2012), https://www.sog .unc.edu/sites/default/files/course_materials/public_records_overview.pdf (updated and revised from a previous paper authored by David M. Lawrence).

A board member may be found *personally* liable for all or part of the attorney's fees owed to a plaintiff if the court finds that the board member knowingly or intentionally committed, caused, permitted, suborned, or participated in a violation of the public records law. However, a board member cannot be held personally liable for such fees if the board member sought and followed the advice of an attorney with respect to the public records request at issue.[22] Because of this potential shield from personal liability, it is prudent for board members to consult with an attorney when deciding whether to withhold records in response to a public records request.

Records Retention Requirements

Public officials, including social services board members, are prohibited from destroying, selling, loaning, or disposing of any public record except as allowed by a records retention and disposition schedule established by the North Carolina Department of Natural and Cultural Resources (NC DNCR).[23] These schedules determine how long certain categories of records must be retained and when they may be disposed of or destroyed. The current retention and disposition schedules for local governments are available on NC DNCR's website.[24]

Many of a social services board's records (such as meeting minutes) fall under categories described in the general records schedule for local government agencies. That schedule must be approved by the BOCC. The social services board should obtain a copy of the county's approved general records schedule to ensure that social services board members are properly preserving and disposing of records.

The records of a county DSS fall under the records retention and disposition schedule for county social services agencies. The governing board for social services (which may be a county board of social services, a CHS board, or the BOCC) and the director of social services must sign the schedule to acknowledge that they agree to comply with its requirements.[25] That acknowledgement should be made in a regular meeting and recorded as an action in the board's meeting minutes. A signed copy of the signature page must be sent to the NC DNCR Records Analysis Unit, Government Records Section, 4615 Mail Service Center, Raleigh, NC 27699-4615 or faxed to 919-715-3627. If board members are unsure whether NC DNCR has a signed copy of the schedule for their county on file, they may contact a records management analyst at NC DNCR for confirmation.[26]

Notes

1. Chapter 132, Section 1 of the North Carolina General Statutes (hereinafter G.S.).
2. G.S. 132-1(a).
3. *See* Frayda S. Bluestein, Public Records in North Carolina, UNC School of Government (2012), https://www.sog.unc.edu/sites/default/files/course_materials/public_records_overview.pdf (updated and revised from a previous paper authored by David M. Lawrence).
4. G.S. 132-6(a).
5. G.S. 132-6(a).
6. Kristi A. Nickodem & Kristina Wilson, *Responding to First Amendment "Audits" in the Local Government Context,* Loc. Gov't L. Bull. No. 141 (Nov. 2022), 62, https://www.sog.unc.edu/sites/default/files/reports/2022-11-09%2020220124%20LGLB%20141.pdf.
7. G.S. 132-6(a1).
8. *See* Bluestein, *supra* note 3.
9. *See* G.S. 108A, §§ 80, 11. Other statutes and regulations also make specific types of social services and public assistance information confidential.
10. G.S. 143-318.10(c).
11. G.S. 153A-98(a).
12. G.S. 132-1.1(a).
13. G.S. 132-1.10(b)(5).
14. *See* G.S. 132-6(c).
15. *See* G.S. 132-6.2(e).
16. G.S. 153A-98(b).
17. G.S. 132-6(a); G.S. 132-2.
18. For a discussion regarding problems with the records-custodian concept as it is defined in the public records law, see Frayda Bluestein, *Custodians of Public Records,* Coates' Canons: NC Loc. Gov't L. (blog) (Dec. 19, 2014), https://canons.sog.unc.edu/2014/12/custodians-of-public-records/.
19. G.S. 132-9(a).
20. G.S. 132-9(c).
21. *Id.*
22. *Id.*
23. G.S. 132-3(a); G.S. 121-5.
24. *Local Government Agencies,* State Archives of N.C. (last visited Apr. 4, 2023), https://archives.ncdcr.gov/government/local.
25. *Id.; see also* G.S. 121-5(c).
26. *See Directory of Records Management Analysts for Local Government Agencies,* State Archives of N.C. (last visited Apr. 4, 2023), https://archives.ncdcr.gov/government/local/analysts.

Chapter 15

Legal Liability and Immunity

The actions of a county social services agency or its governing board may subject a county to liability in a variety of ways. In many cases, it is the county itself that is liable for legal claims involving social services officials and employees. However, in some cases, a lawsuit may also seek to hold individual social services board members, the social services director, or social services employees personally liable for their conduct. While lawsuits against social services boards and board members are relatively rare, the actions of a county social services agency's director or employees are a more frequent source of litigation.

This chapter will discuss the ways in which liability can arise from lawsuits related to social services, the types of immunity available to the county and board members, and the board's role in helping to reduce the risks of such liability for the county.[1]

Lawsuits Against Board Members

An individual may file a civil lawsuit against social services board members in either their official capacities or their individual capacities. Alternatively, an individual may bring legal claims against board members in *both* their official and individual capacities. The difference between *official capacity claims* and *individual capacity claims* is a big one. It determines who is potentially liable for damages in the lawsuit and what types of immunity are available to the named board members.

Official Capacity Claims

If a person sues a board member in the member's official capacity based on the board's alleged violation of state or federal law, the lawsuit is, in essence, a lawsuit against the *county*.[2] Even though individual board members are named as defendants, an official capacity lawsuit does not seek to hold the individual board members liable. This means that if a monetary judgment is entered against board members in their official capacities, the legal responsibility for paying the judgment lies with the county and not with the individual board members. Likewise, if the director of social services is sued in the director's official capacity, the lawsuit seeks to recover monetary damages from the county, not the director personally.

If an official capacity lawsuit is filed against social services board members, the board and the affected members should immediately contact the county attorney regarding the lawsuit.

Individual Capacity Claims

By contrast, a lawsuit that names a board member in the member's individual capacity is alleging that the board member is *personally* liable.[3] This means that if a monetary judgment is entered against the board member, the legal responsibility for paying the judgment lies with the individual board member, not the county. Likewise, if the director of social services is sued in the director's individual capacity, the lawsuit is seeking to hold the director personally liable for a violation of the law.

If a lawsuit names a board member as a defendant in the member's individual capacity, the board member may want to consider seeking advice from independent legal counsel.

Lawsuits Against the County

In North Carolina, a county social services agency is a subdivision of a county government, not a separate or independent legal entity.[4] Consequently, if a lawsuit is brought against a county social services agency, it is the county, not the agency itself, that is the proper defendant.[5] This means that counties may, in some circumstances, be subject to liability based on the acts or omissions of county social services employees, including the director of social services.

In recent years, lawsuits against North Carolina counties based on allegations involving county social services agencies have led to substantial awards of monetary damages and high-profile media coverage.[6] Social services board members can help lower the risk of such lawsuits by maintaining an open dialogue with the social services director regarding problems affecting the department, routinely evaluating the director's performance, and disciplining or dismissing the director if necessary.

Liability Under the Open Meetings Law and Public Records Law

Please refer to Chapter 13 for information about liability under the open meetings law and Chapter 14 for information about liability under the public records law. If a social services board member knowingly and intentionally violates the open meetings law or the public records law, a court may order the board member to personally pay all or part of a plaintiff's attorney's fees.[7] However, a board member cannot be held personally liable for such fees under either law if the board member sought and followed the advice of an attorney with respect to the action or request at issue.[8]

Liability and Immunity for Tort Claims

Sometimes lawsuits involving county social services agencies turn on a question of tort liability. A tort is a wrongful act or omission (other than a criminal act or breach of contract) that causes some form of harm or injury and for which courts will provide a remedy (typically in the form of monetary damages).[9]

To succeed in a tort lawsuit, the injured party (the plaintiff) must generally demonstrate that a defendant violated a duty owed to the plaintiff and that the violation caused harm to the plaintiff or the plaintiff's property.[10]

This section discusses tort claims brought against counties and county officials. However, board members should also be aware that the State Tort Claims Act allows the North Carolina Department of Health and Human Services to be held liable based on the negligence of a county DSS director or employee if the director or employee was acting as an "agent of the State" when the alleged negligence occurred.[11]

Categories of Torts

There are two primary categories of torts.[12]

Negligence torts involve a failure to exercise the standard of care that a reasonably prudent person would have exercised in a similar situation.[13] A person may only be liable for negligence if that person had a duty to act according to a particular standard of care, failed to do so, and thereby caused harm to another person or property. For example, a social services agency and its employees might face a lawsuit based on

- negligent placement of a child in a foster or adoptive home,[14]
- negligent assessment of a report of abuse or neglect,[15]
- negligence in acting as a guardian for a legally incompetent adult,[16]
- negligent infliction of emotional distress,[17] or
- negligent hiring, retention, or supervision of an employee.[18]

Intentional torts, by contrast, are committed by someone acting with intent to engage in a wrongful act.[19] Examples of intentional torts include battery (nonconsensual touching of the body of another with the intent to cause harmful or offensive contact), intentional infliction of emotional distress, and defamation.

Governmental Immunity for Tort Claims Against the County

In North Carolina, when a lawsuit is brought against a county, a legal doctrine known as *governmental immunity* protects the county from liability for tort claims so long as (1) the claim arises from the performance of governmental (as opposed to proprietary) functions, and (2) the county has not waived its immunity through the purchase of liability insurance.[20] Most, if not all, of the activities performed by county departments of social services, social services employees, and social services board members are governmental in nature, meaning that the county will generally be shielded from liability for tort claims arising from those activities.[21]

As discussed earlier in this chapter, legal claims against the county DSS or the social services board, as well as legal claims against a DSS director or board member in their "official capacities," are all in essence lawsuits against the county itself.[22] This means that governmental immunity applies to tort claims against any of these parties as long as the claims arise from the performance of governmental functions, unless the county has waived such immunity.[23] Governmental immunity does not apply to social services board members in the rare instances when they are sued in their *individual* capacities, but as discussed in the following section, "public official" immunity may apply to those claims.[24]

Public Official Immunity from Tort Claims Against Board Members and DSS Directors

If a social services board member or DSS director is sued in their individual capacity, a legal doctrine known as "public official immunity" may apply. It protects a public official (including a social services board member or director of social services) from personal liability for claims alleging negligence in the exercise of the judgment and discretion with which the official is invested by virtue of the office.[25] However, this immunity is not absolute.

Public official immunity does not apply if the board member's or DSS director's "act, or failure to act, was corrupt or malicious" or if the board member or DSS director "acted outside of and beyond the scope of his duties."[26] Additionally, some North Carolina Court of Appeals decisions have held that public official immunity applies only to mere negligence claims, meaning it does not protect board members or DSS directors who are sued in their individual capacities for *intentional* torts.[27]

Limitations to Governmental Immunity and Public Official Immunity

It is important to remember that governmental immunity and public official immunity apply only to tort claims. These immunity doctrines do not protect the county, a board member, or a DSS director from legal claims alleging

- breach of a valid contract;[28]
- violations of a person's rights under the United States Constitution (see below);
- violations of federal law, such as Title VII of the Civil Rights Act of 1964, the Americans with Disabilities Act, the Age Discrimination in Employment Act, or federal criminal laws; or
- violations of state law, such as the public records law, the open meetings law, social services confidentiality statutes (e.g., G.S. 108A-80), or state criminal laws.

Liability and Immunity for Claims Under 42 U.S.C. 1983

Sometimes a lawsuit against a social services agency alleges a violation of an individual's rights under the United States Constitution. In such a case, the claim is typically brought under 42 U.S.C. § 1983 (often called *Section 1983*), a federal statute that authorizes a person to sue and receive injunctive relief or monetary damages from a local government or local government official if the government's conduct or public official's conduct violates the person's rights under the United States Constitution or certain federal statutes.[29]

County social services officials and employees may be sued for prospective injunctive relief under Section 1983 (typically meaning the suit seeks a court order stopping the agency's officials and employees from engaging in certain conduct in the future). Under certain circumstances, counties may also be held liable for monetary damages in Section 1983 lawsuits that involve the conduct of county social services officials or employees.[30] Section 1983 lawsuits frequently allege violations of federal constitutional rights, such as the First Amendment right to free speech or the Fourteenth Amendment right of due process.

Section 1983 claims may be brought against public officials or public employees in their individual capacities. Social services board members are rarely sued under Section 1983,[31] but it is more common for DSS directors and employees to face individual capacity claims under Section 1983.[32] Board members and DSS directors, like other public officials, may be held personally liable for monetary damages under Section 1983 when sued in their individual capacities. However, a legal doctrine known as *qualified immunity* frequently protects them from personal liability. Qualified immunity protects public officials and employees from personal liability under Section 1983 so long as their conduct "does not violate clearly established statutory or constitutional rights of which a reasonable person would have known."[33] A right is clearly established when it is "sufficiently clear that every reasonable official would have understood that what he is doing violates that right."[34] This means that qualified immunity generally protects social services board members, DSS directors, and DSS employees from personal liability under Section 1983 unless they are "plainly incompetent or . . . knowingly violate the law."[35]

Criminal Liability

Social services board members and county social services directors are subject to generally applicable federal and state criminal laws, as well as to certain criminal laws that specifically govern the conduct of public officials. For example, a social services board member or a county social services director may be held criminally liable for

- unlawfully disclosing confidential information regarding persons who have applied for or are receiving public assistance or social services from the county social services department;[36]
- unlawfully receiving a direct benefit from a contract that involves the county social services department (see Chapter 12);[37]
- receiving a gift, service, favor, or reward in return for attempting to influence the award of a contract by the county social services department (see Chapter 12);[38]

- willfully disrupting an official meeting of the county social services board or another public body;[39]
- assaulting other social services board members, the county social services director, a social services employee, or other individuals;[40]
- embezzling or willfully and corruptly misapplying county funds;[41]
- making a false statement under oath in the context of a lawsuit;[42] or
- willfully failing to discharge duties as a public official.[43]

Lawsuits Related to the DSS Director's Employment

Civil lawsuits regarding the actions or omissions of county social services boards are rare, but they sometimes are filed in response to the board's alleged violation of the State Human Resources Act or federal antidiscrimination laws in connection with the board's recruitment, selection, discipline, or dismissal of the social services director.[44] A county may also face a lawsuit based on allegations that the social services board negligently hired and retained the social services director.[45]

Actions taken with respect to the DSS director's employment, including the hiring process, are the most likely source of potential litigation for the board. Accordingly, the board should be particularly careful to

- document all actions with respect to the DSS director's employment, including documenting concerns about the director's performance or conduct and the steps the board took to address those concerns; and
- seek guidance regarding applicable state and federal employment laws when recruiting, selecting, disciplining, or dismissing the director.

Legal Representation and Indemnification of Public Officials

Legal Representation

A county is authorized, but not required, to provide legal representation for a social services board member in connection with any civil or criminal action brought against the board member on account of alleged acts or omissions committed in the scope and course of the board member's service on the board.[46] Likewise, a county is authorized, not required, to provide legal representation for a county DSS director in connection with any civil or criminal action brought against the director on account of alleged acts or omissions committed in the scope and course of the director's employment.

The county may provide this representation through its own attorney, through a private attorney, or by purchasing insurance that requires the insurer to provide the defense.[47] The board of county commissioners is responsible for deciding whether or not to provide such legal representation to an individual public official.

Liability Insurance

State law authorizes counties to purchase insurance to protect any of their officers, agents, or employees from civil liability for damages arising from acts or omissions within the scope of their authority and the course of their employment.[48] The board of county commissioners has discretion to determine what claims and which public officials and employees will be covered by this liability insurance.[49] This means that counties may choose to purchase insurance that protects social services board members from individual civil liability in connection with their board service (or that protects the DSS director from individual civil liability in connection with the director's employment), but counties are not required to purchase such insurance.

Paying Settlements or Judgments

Each county is authorized, but not required, to pay all or part of any settlement or judgment entered in a lawsuit brought against a current or former county official (including a county social services board member) on account of alleged acts or omissions within the scope of the official's public office if the following conditions are met:

1. notice of the legal claim or litigation is given to the board of county commissioners prior to the time that the claim is settled or civil judgment is entered;
2. the county has adopted a set of uniform standards (made available for public inspection) under which settlements or judgments against county officials will be paid; and
3. the board of county commissioners determines that the county official did not act or fail to act because of actual fraud, corruption, or actual malice.[50]

Notes

1. The legal liability and immunity of state and county social services agencies, officials, and employees is discussed in more detail in JOHN L. SAXON, SOCIAL SERVICES IN NORTH CAROLINA ch. 14 (UNC School of Government, 2008). The legal liability and immunity of North Carolina local governments, officials, and employees is also discussed in Anthony Baker, *Civil Liability of the Local Government and Its Officials and Employees, in* COUNTY AND MUNICIPAL GOVERNMENT IN NORTH CAROLINA ch. 6 (Frayda S. Bluestein ed., UNC School of Government, 2d ed. 2014).
2. *See* Meyer v. Walls, 347 N.C. 97, 110 (1997) ("A suit against a defendant in his individual capacity means that the plaintiff seeks recovery from the defendant directly; a suit against a defendant in his official capacity means that the plaintiff seeks recovery from the entity of which the public servant defendant is an agent.").
3. *Id.*
4. *See, e.g., Meyer,* 347 N.C. 97; Malloy v. Durham Cnty. Dep't of Soc. Servs., 58 N.C. App. 61 (1982) (county DSS has no capacity to sue or be sued).
5. *See Meyer,* 347 N.C. 97 (an action against a county DSS that directly affects the rights of the county is an action against the county); Johnson v. Marrow, 228 N.C. 58 (a county must be sued for the acts of its agencies); *see also* Wade v. Alamance Cnty. Dep't of Soc. Servs., No. 1:19-CV-619, 2020 WL 3846336, at *5 (M.D.N.C. July 8, 2020) (compiling cases in which federal district courts in North Carolina have dismissed claims against county departments of social services); West v. Buncombe Cnty., No. 1:14-CV-00088-MOC-DSC, 2014 WL 4384021, at *3 (W.D.N.C. Sept. 3, 2014) (dismissing claims asserted against a consolidated human services agency on grounds that the entity lacked legal capacity for suit).
6. *See, e.g.,* Kate Martin, *NC County Settles Child Removal Lawsuits for $42 Million,* CAROLINA PUB. PRESS, June 30, 2022, https://carolinapublicpress.org/55049/nc-county-settles-child-removal-lawsuits-for-42-million/; Lizzie Presser, *How 'Shadow' Foster Care is Tearing Families Apart,* N.Y. TIMES MAG., Dec. 2, 2021, https://www.nytimes.com/2021/12/01/magazine/shadow-foster-care.html.
7. G.S. 132-9(c); G.S. 143-318.16B.
8. G.S. 132-9(c); G.S. 143-318.16B.
9. *Tort,* BLACK'S LAW DICTIONARY (11th ed. 2019).
10. *See* Anthony J. Baker, *Civil Liability of the Local Government and Its Officials and Employees, in* COUNTY AND MUNICIPAL GOVERNMENT IN NORTH CAROLINA 95 (Frayda S. Bluestein ed., UNC School of Government, 2d ed. 2014).
11. *See* SAXON, *supra* note 1, at 252 (citing Gammons v. N.C. Dep't of Hum. Res., 344 N.C. 51 (1996); Vaughn v. N.C. Dep't of Hum. Res., 296 N.C. 683 (1979)); *see also* G.S. 143-291 (the State Tort Claims Act); G.S. 108A-14 (responsibility of DSS director to act as an agent of NCDHHS with respect to certain work).
12. A third category of torts, known as strict-liability torts, is beyond the scope of this chapter.
13. *See Negligence,* BLACK'S LAW DICTIONARY (11th ed. 2019).
14. White v. Stokes Cnty. Dep't of Soc. Servs., 207 N.C. App. 378 (2010); Hobbs *ex rel.* Winner v. N.C. Dep't of Hum. Res., 135 N.C. App. 412 (1999).
15. *See, e.g.,* Hunter v. Transylvania Cnty. Dep't of Soc. Servs., 207 N.C. App. 735 (2010); Whitaker v. Clark, 109 N.C. App. 379 (1993).
16. Meyer v. Walls, 347 N.C. 97 (1997).

17. *See* McConnell v. Watauga Cnty., No. 5:17-CV-195-MOC-DCK, 2019 WL 2344223 (W.D.N.C. May 31, 2019), *aff'd*, 790 F. App'x 543 (4th Cir. 2020).

18. *See* Christmas v. Cabarrus Cnty., 192 N.C. App. 227 (2008).

19. *See Tort*, Black's Law Dictionary (11th ed. 2019).

20. *See* Trey Allen, Local Government Immunity to Lawsuits in North Carolina 2 (UNC School of Government, 2018).

21. Saxon, *supra* note 1, at 255.

22. *See, e.g.*, Meyer v. Walls, 347 N.C. 97, 110 (1997); Malloy v. Durham Cnty. Dep't of Soc. Servs., 58 N.C. App. 61, 67 (1982); Avery v. Burke Cnty., 660 F.2d 111, 114 (4th Cir. 1981) ("Neither the Board of Health nor the Board of Social Services is a legal entity separate and apart from the county. Both boards are created by, and are extensions of, the county."); *see also* Johnson v. Marrow, 228 N.C. 58, 59 (1947) ("Where a county is the real party in interest, it must sue and be sued in its name."). G.S. 153A–11 establishes that a county is a legal entity which may be sued, but there is no state statute authorizing lawsuits against a county DSS or social services board.

23. For more information about the waiver of governmental immunity, please see Allen, *supra* note 20, ch. 4.

24. *See* Wright v. Gaston Cnty., 205 N.C. App. 600 (2010) ("Plaintiff's complaint also alleges claims against the [defendants] in their individual capacities, for which governmental immunity is not applicable.").

25. Hart v. Brienza, 246 N.C. App. 426, 431 (2016) (quoting Smith v. State, 289 N.C. 303, 331 (1976)); *see also* Hunter v. Transylvania Cnty. Dep't of Soc. Servs., 207 N.C. App. 735, 738 (2010) ("The director of social services has long been recognized as a public official.").

26. Doe v. Wake Cnty., 264 N.C. App. 692, 695, (2019) (quoting Hobbs *ex rel.* Winner v. N.C. Dep't of Hum. Res., 135 N.C. App. 412, 422 (1999)).

27. *See* McCullers v. Lewis, 265 N.C. App. 216, 222 (2019); Wells v. N.C. Dep't of Corr., 152 N.C. App. 307, 320 (2002). For a more comprehensive discussion of this topic, please see Trey Allen, *Do Intentional Tort Claims Always Defeat Public Official Immunity?*, Loc. Gov't L. Bull. No. 139 (UNC School of Government, Sept. 2016); *see also* Trey Allen, *Public Official Immunity for Intentional Torts? The Split Continues*, Coates' Canons: NC Loc. Gov't L. (blog) (June 20, 2019), https://canons.sog.unc.edu/2019/06/public-official-immunity-for-intentional-torts-the-split-continues/.

28. *See* Wray v. City of Greensboro, 370 N.C. 41, 47 (2017). Entering into a valid contract constitutes a waiver of governmental immunity.

29. The legal liability of North Carolina local governments and local government officials and employees under Section 1983 is discussed in Baker, *supra* note 1.

30. *See* Monell v. Dep't of Soc. Servs. of N.Y., 436 U.S. 658 (1978); *see also* Hogan v. Cherokee Cnty., 519 F. Supp. 3d 263 (W.D.N.C. 2021).

31. *See generally* Hunt v. Robeson Cnty. Dep't of Soc. Servs., 816 F.2d 150 (4th Cir. 1987); Avery v. Burke Cnty., 660 F.2d 111 (4th Cir. 1981); Blanks v. Register, 493 F.2d 697 (4th Cir. 1974); Fracaro v. Priddy, 514 F. Supp. 191 (M.D.N.C. 1981).

32. *See, e.g.*, Evans v. Perry, 578 F. App'x 229 (4th Cir. 2014); Booker v. S.C. Dep't of Soc. Servs., 583 F. App'x 147 (4th Cir. 2014); *Hogan*, 519 F. Supp. 3d 263; Olavarria v. North Carolina, No. 5:19-CV-162-FL, 2020 WL 5939087 (E.D.N.C. Jan. 2, 2020); Shupe v. Baur, No. 7:14-CV-56-F, 2015 WL 2193794 (E.D.N.C. May 11, 2015).

33. Mullenix v. Luna, 577 U.S. 7, 11 (2015) (citing Pearson v. Callahan, 555 U.S. 223, 231 (2009)).

34. *Id.* at 11 (quoting Reichle v. Howards, 566 U.S. 658 (2012)).

35. *Id.* at 12 (quoting Malley v. Briggs, 475 U.S. 335, 341 (1986)).

36. G.S. 108A-80.

37. G.S. 14-234. Chapter 12 discusses this statute in more detail.

38. *Id.* Chapter 12 discusses this statute in more detail.

39. G.S. 143-318.17.

40. *See, e.g.,* G.S. 14, §§ 33, 34.2, 32.4.
41. G.S. 14-92.
42. G.S. 14-209.
43. G.S. 14-230(a).
44. *See, e.g.,* Fields v. Prater, 566 F.3d 381 (4th Cir. 2009); Bockes v. Fields, 999 F.2d 788, 791 (4th Cir. 1993); Fuqua v. Rockingham Cnty. Bd. of Soc. Servs., 125 N.C. App. 66 (1997); Dial v. Robeson Cnty., No. 1:20-CV-1135, 2021 WL 4460320, *2 (M.D.N.C. Sept. 29, 2021); Blanks v. Register, No. 1610, 1973 WL 317 (E.D.N.C. May 14, 1973).
45. *See* Hogan v. Cherokee Cnty., 519 F. Supp. 3d 263 (W.D.N.C. 2021); *see also* Hogan v. Cherokee Cnty., No. 1:18-CV-96, 2019 WL 2591089 (W.D.N.C. Feb. 28), *report and recommendation adopted,* No. 1:18-CV-00096-MR-WCM, 2019 WL 1376074 (W.D.N.C. Mar. 27, 2019).
46. *See* G.S. 160A-167(a); G.S. 153A-97.
47. G.S. 160A-167(a).
48. G.S. 153A-435.
49. G.S. 153A-435(a).
50. G.S. 160A, § 167(b), (c).

Chapter 16

Consolidated Human Services Agencies and Boards

Since 2012, all North Carolina counties with a county manager have had authority to create consolidated human services agencies (CHSAs).[1] Prior to 2012, this option was only available to counties with populations of over 425,000 people.[2] As of the time this book goes to print, thirty counties provide social services through a CHSA, including many of North Carolina's most populous counties. This chapter provides a basic overview of the laws pertaining to CHSAs and their governing boards.

Key Differences Between a CHSA and a Standalone County DSS

Appointment and Supervision of the Director

The most significant difference between a CHSA and a standalone (nonconsolidated) department of social services is that the consolidated human services (CHS) director is appointed by the county manager, not by the governing board.[3] However, the governing board for the CHSA (which can be the county commissioners or an appointed board) must provide advice on the appointment and consent to the appointment. The CHS director also reports to the county manager, unlike a traditional DSS director.

Staff Hiring Authority

Another important difference is that the CHS director may only hire CHSA staff with the approval of the county manager, whereas a county director of social services has sole authority to make all hiring decisions for a county DSS.[4]

Personnel Rules and Policies

The other key difference between a CHSA and a standalone county DSS is that CHSA employees are no longer covered by the State Human Resource Act (SHRA) and instead become subject solely to county personnel policies when the CHSA is created, unless the board of county commissioners (BOCC) affirmatively elects to keep them under the SHRA.[5] To date, the majority of North Carolina counties with a CHSA have opted to remove CHSA employees from the coverage of the SHRA.

Structure of a CHSA

State law authorizes each BOCC to create a CHSA to "carry out the functions of any combination of commissions, boards, or agencies appointed by the board of county commissioners or acting under and pursuant to the authority of the board of county commissioners."[6] Counties can choose which "human services" functions to include in a CHSA. The term *human services* is undefined in the law, which gives counties some flexibility as to which functions to include in the new agency. A CHSA may incorporate a local health department and/or county DSS, but other departments and agencies may also be involved (such as local departments focused on veterans, aging populations, or transportation).

There are, however, some limitations. A CHSA may *not* include:

- A local management entity (LME) involved with mental health, developmental disabilities, and substance abuse (MH/DD/SA) services, with the exception of the CHSA in Mecklenburg County;[7]
- A public health authority assigned the power, duties, and responsibilities to provide public health services as outlined in G.S. 130A-1.1;[8]
- A public hospital authority authorized to provide public health services under S.L. 1997-502;[9] or
- A public hospital as defined in G.S. 159-39(a).[10]

To date, all CHSAs formed in North Carolina have incorporated a county DSS. Most CHSAs, but not all, have also incorporated the local health department.[11]

A CHSA can be governed by an appointed CHS board or governed directly by the BOCC.[12] Both governance options are discussed in more detail in this chapter.

Table 16.1 lists some differences between a county DSS and a CHSA.

CHSA Governance Option 1: Board of County Commissioners

The BOCC has the option of serving directly as the governing board for a CHSA.[13] If the BOCC plans to serve as the governing board for a CHSA, it must hold a public hearing and give at least thirty days' notice of the hearing in a newspaper having general circulation in the county.[14] The hearing requirement is triggered by the BOCC assuming the powers and duties of another board, which could be a local board of health, a county board of social services, or a CHS board. Following the public hearing, the BOCC may adopt a resolution "assuming and conferring upon the board of county commissioners all powers, responsibilities and duties" of the governing board for social services and/or the local board of health.[15]

A BOCC that abolishes the governing board for social services takes on all the responsibilities of the social services board (with the exception of appointing the

Table 16.1. Differences Between a County DSS and a CHSA

	County DSS	CHSA
Who appoints and dismisses the agency's director?	Board of social services (which may be the BOCC)	County manager, with the advice and consent of the agency's governing board (which may be the BOCC)
Who has authority to hire agency staff?	County DSS director	CHS director, with the approval of the county manager
Does the SHRA apply to agency employees?	Yes	No, unless BOCC opts to keep employees subject to the SHRA
Who may serve as the agency's governing board?	Appointed board of social services or BOCC	Appointed CHS board or BOCC

Note: DSS = department of social services; CHSA = consolidated human services agency; BOCC = board of county commissioners; CHS = consolidated human services; SHRA = State Human Resources Act.

agency director), including the board's responsibilities related to social services policy and administration described in Chapter 9. Likewise, if the BOCC becomes the governing body for a CHSA that includes public health, it will assume almost all the responsibilities of a local board of health, including acting as the adjudicatory body for public health, imposing certain fees for public health services, public health rulemaking, and taking on activities necessary for state accreditation of the health department.[16]

If the CHSA includes public health and the BOCC assumes the powers and duties of the governing board, the BOCC must appoint an advisory committee for public health.[17] The advisory committee must, at a minimum, include members representing all of the required categories of membership for a county board of health, which are found in G.S. 130A-35.[18] There is no corresponding legal requirement to create a social services advisory committee. However, a BOCC has the *option* of appointing an advisory committee for social services. The BOCC could either expand the public health advisory committee to include members with social services expertise or appoint a separate advisory committee for social services, but neither option is required by law.[19]

Advisory committees are, as the name suggests, purely advisory in nature.[20] An advisory committee cannot exercise all of the powers and duties of a CHS board. Rather, the committee serves to advise the county commissioners on matters that require public health or human services expertise. If a BOCC chooses to act as the governing board for a CHSA, it cannot delegate its authority to the advisory committee to carry out key public health duties, such as setting fees for public health services, adopting local public health rules, or adjudicating disputes. North Carolina's accreditation standards for local health departments (including CHSAs) allow the BOCC to delegate only a limited set of responsibilities to the public health advisory committee, such as reviewing and reporting on community health assessment data, receiving community input, informing public officials about community health issues, fostering community partnerships, and advocating for financial resources for the agency.[21]

Advisory committees are public bodies subject to North Carolina's open meetings law[22] and public records law[23] (see Chapters 13 and 14). The state statute that creates the advisory-committee requirement, G.S 153A-77(a), leaves a number of unanswered questions about advisory committees. It does not prescribe how often the committee should meet, whether the committee should have a chair, who can call a special meeting of the committee, or when a committee member may be removed. Advisory committees could look to the statute governing county boards of health (G.S. 130A-35) for guidance on these matters, but the statute is not binding as to advisory committees.[24] Accordingly, advisory committees should consider creating their own rules of procedure to address these questions.

CHSA Governance Option 2: Appointed CHS Board

If a BOCC does not want to serve as the governing board of the CHSA, it must appoint a CHS board.

The BOCC must first create a nominating committee consisting of members of the current (preconsolidation) board of health and social services board, as well as the board responsible for managing MH/DD/SA services in the county.[25] The nominating committee recommends members for the new CHS board, and the BOCC must make appointments based upon those recommendations. After the initial board is in place, the BOCC fills CHS board vacancies based upon nominees presented by the members of the CHS board.

The initial CHS board could, in theory, include members from the existing board of health and social services board, provided that those individuals otherwise meet the membership qualifications described below. Including some preconsolidation board members could help to provide some continuity in board operations when the CHS board is first formed. However, in some situations, retaining the existing, preconsolidation board members may not serve the county's goals in creating the CHSA and the CHS board.

Composition of the CHS Board

The CHS board must be composed of no more than twenty-five members. All members of the CHS board must be residents of the county in which the CHSA is located.[26]

The composition of the CHS board must reasonably reflect the population makeup of the county and must include

- four people who are consumers of human services;[27]
- eight professionals, each with qualifications in one of these categories: one psychologist, one pharmacist, one engineer, one dentist, one optometrist, one veterinarian, one social worker, and one registered nurse;[28]

- two physicians licensed to practice medicine in North Carolina, one of whom must be a psychiatrist;
- one county commissioner; and
- other persons, including "members of the general public representing various occupations."[29]

The BOCC may appoint a member of the CHS board to concurrently fill more than one category of membership (the categories described above) if the member has the qualifications or attributes of more than one category of membership.[30] For example, if a candidate for board membership is a registered nurse and a consumer of human services, that single individual could fulfill requirements for representation of both those categories on the board.

What happens when there are no county residents who fulfill one of the categories described above available to serve on the board? The CHS board statute does not answer this question.[31] If no county resident is available to serve in one of the licensed professional positions, then that seat on the CHS board likely must remain temporarily vacant. The BOCC and the CHS board should, however, continue to make diligent efforts to recruit CHS board members who will fulfill all of the required categories of membership.

The statute also leaves another unanswered question: Who is a "consumer of human services"? The term *human services* is not defined under state law, which means counties have some leeway to interpret the concept. A cautious interpretation would be to treat *human service* as a service, benefit, or program that is provided by the CHSA in the county. However, the term could be interpreted more broadly. For example, a consumer of mental health services, substance abuse treatment services, or developmental disability services could be considered a consumer of human services, even though those services may not be provided directly by a CHSA. Some counties have also interpreted the category to include parents whose children receive "human services" (for example, a parent whose child has a developmental disability or a parent whose child receives services through the health department).

Terms and Term Limits

In general, CHS board members are appointed to serve four-year terms.[32] However, for purposes of establishing a uniform staggered term structure for the board, the BOCC may appoint some members for less than a four-year term when the CHS board is initially formed.

A member may not serve more than two consecutive four-year terms on the CHS board.[33] A county commissioner may serve on the CHS board only as long as the individual is a county commissioner.[34] This is different from a county board of social services, where a commissioner's term on the board is not tied to or affected by the individual's tenure or term as a county commissioner.

Board Business

Board chair and secretary. The CHS board must elect a board member to serve as chair on an annual basis. The CHS director serves as the executive officer of the CHS board, but only to the extent and in the manner authorized by the county manager.[35]

Quorum. A majority of the actual membership constitutes a quorum for purposes of conducting business as a CHS board.[36]

Meetings. A CHS board must meet at least quarterly. The board chair or three of the board members may call a special meeting.[37]

Per diem. Board members may receive a per diem in an amount established by the BOCC.[38] The BOCC also has authority to set a policy for reimbursement of CHS board members for subsistence and travel.

Removal of a CHS Board Member

The BOCC has authority to remove a CHS board member from the CHS board if the member has

1. committed a felony or other crime involving moral turpitude;
2. violated a state law governing conflicts of interest;
3. violated a written policy adopted by the BOCC;
4. habitually failed to attend meetings;
5. engaged in conduct that tends to bring the office into disrepute; or
6. failed to maintain qualifications required for appointment to the CHS board (such as county residency or professional qualifications).[39]

A CHS board member may be removed only after the member has been given written notice of the basis for removal and has had the opportunity to respond.[40]

Powers and Duties of the CHS Board

The governing board for a CHSA—which could be the BOCC or an appointed CHS board—has a number of responsibilities established by state law. Some, but not all, of these responsibilities are derived from the CHS board's role as a governing board for social services and/or public health.

Social Services and Public Health Powers and Duties

When county departments or functions are consolidated into a CHSA, the governing board for each previously separate agency (the county board of social services and/or county board of health) is abolished. With a few exceptions, the governing board for the CHSA assumes all the powers and duties of the governing boards that were abolished when the CHSA was created.

Social Services

If the CHSA includes social services, the CHS board acquires all powers and duties of the county board of social services except (1) appointing the agency director and (2) transmitting or presenting the social services budget to the BOCC.[41] The CHS board's acquired powers and duties include the responsibilities related to social services policy and administration described in Chapter 9.

Public Health

If the CHSA includes public health, the CHS board acquires all powers and duties of the local board of health except (1) appointing the agency director and (2) transmitting or presenting the budget for local health programs to the BOCC.[42]

The public health powers and duties acquired by the CHS board include the authority and responsibility to

- adopt local health rules,[43]
- conduct hearings in appeals of local health rule enforcement actions,[44]
- perform regulatory health functions required by state law,[45] and
- impose fees for certain public health services offered by the CHSA (subject to constraints in the law).[46]

The CHS board must also perform certain activities required for health department accreditation. All local health departments in North Carolina—including CHSAs—must obtain and maintain accreditation by satisfying accreditation standards adopted by the North Carolina Local Health Department Accreditation Board and applicable rules adopted by the North Carolina Commission for Public Health.[47] The accreditation rules include benchmarks specifically related to the local board of health's activities.[48] Among other things, these benchmarks include training requirements for the board.[49] Members of the CHS board should learn about these benchmarks through reading the most recent Health Department Self-Assessment Instrument (HDSAI) Interpretation Document released by the North Carolina Local Health Department Accreditation Program.[50]

Other Powers and Duties of the CHS Board

In addition to the powers and duties of a county board of social services and/or county board of health, state law gives CHS boards a number of other powers and duties described below.

Ensuring compliance. The CHS board is responsible for ensuring the CHSA's compliance with laws related to state and federal programs.[51] State law gives the CHS board authority to conduct audits and reviews of human services programs, including quality assurance activities, when required by state and federal law or periodically as the board may deem necessary.[52] However, in some circumstances, the CHS director's ability to share information about individual cases with the board may be limited by federal and state confidentiality laws (see Chapter 9).

Recommending new programs. The CHS board may recommend the creation of human services programs.[53] Seeking out information regarding the programs and services offered by the county's CHSA, as well as programs and services offered by other community organizations, will help CHS board members to understand potential gaps in service delivery to community members.

Setting fees for services. The CHS board has authority to set fees for certain services provided by the CHSA, based upon recommendations of the CHS director.[54] Any fees set by the CHS board are subject to the same restrictions on amount and scope that would apply if the fees were set by a county board of health or a county board of social services. The CHS board cannot establish a fee for a service that the CHSA is legally required to provide free of charge. For example, state law prohibits a CHSA from charging a fee for certain public health services, such as sickle-cell-syndrome testing and counseling,[55] examination and treatment for tuberculosis or sexually transmitted diseases,[56] and administration of certain vaccines to children in low-income families who meet specific criteria.[57]

Budget planning. The CHS board is responsible, along with the CHS director, for planning and recommending a CHS budget.[58] However, the CHS board does not have authority or a duty to present or transmit the agency's proposed budget to the BOCC.

Advising local officials. The CHS board advises local officials on health and human services matters *via the county manager*.[59] This is different from county social services boards, who are responsible for *directly* advising county and municipal authorities regarding social services plans and policies.[60] The language of the statute regarding CHS boards suggests that the extent to which the CHS board members advise local officials on health and human services matters is determined by the county manager (and may flow entirely through the county manager).

Public relations and advocacy. The CHS board is responsible for performing public relations and advocacy functions on behalf of the CHSA.[61] This may include advocating at the local, state, and federal level for the adoption, implementation, and funding of plans and policies to address social, economic, and public health problems facing the community. It could also include fostering community partnerships and educating the community about the services and programs offered by the CHSA.

Developing dispute resolution procedures. The CHS board has authority to develop dispute resolution procedures for human services contractors, clients, and public advocates, subject to applicable state and federal dispute resolution procedures for human services programs.[62]

Figure 16.1. Examples of Management Structures for CHSAs

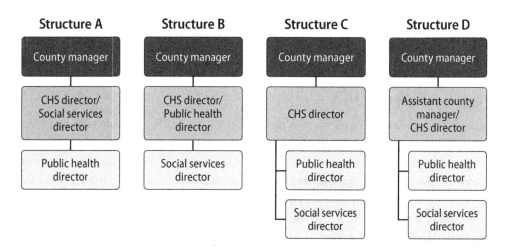

Appointment of the CHS Director and CHSA Organizational Structure

The county manager—not the local governing board—has the power to appoint, dismiss, and supervise the CHS director.[63] However, the county manager's decision to appoint or dismiss the director must be made with the advice and consent of the CHSA's governing board.[64] Unlike a county director of social services or local health director, who has sole authority to hire and fire agency employees, the CHS director may appoint and dismiss CHSA staff only with the county manager's approval.[65]

There are no minimum education or experience requirements for a CHS director set forth in state law. The CHS director will need to be prepared to administer a local agency that carries out numerous state and federal programs and typically has a relatively large budget and staff compared with other local departments.

Except as otherwise provided by law, the individual appointed as the CHS director acquires all of the powers and duties of a social services director and a local health director (if both social services and public health are consolidated into the CHSA).[66] The CHS director is permitted, but not required, to delegate most of these powers and duties to other staff members within the agency.[67]

The county manager and the CHS director have tremendous flexibility in deciding how to structure the internal organization of the CHSA. Figure 16.1 shows some potential management structures for CHSAs. For example, in some counties, the CHS director was formerly a director of social services or local health director prior to consolidation and retains that role after assuming leadership of the CHSA (structures A and B). In other counties, the CHS director designates a social services director and a public health director, who both report to the CHS director and handle the day-to-day management of their respective divisions (structure C). In some counties, an assistant county manager is appointed to be the CHS director and then appoints a social services and a public health director, who report to the assistant county manager (structure D).

There is one limitation on this flexible internal structuring: if the CHS director does not have the statutory qualifications to be a local health director (found in G.S. 130A-40), then the CHS director must appoint a person who has those qualifications and is approved by the county manager.[68]

Employees of the CHSA

Employees of county departments of social services and local health departments are county employees but are subject to the State Human Resources Act (SHRA).[69] When a county creates a new CHSA, the employees of the new agency are removed from SHRA coverage and become subject to county personnel policies, unless the BOCC affirmatively elects to keep them under the SHRA.[70] If the resolution creating the CHSA is silent, then by default, CHSA employees become subject to county personnel policies and are removed from SHRA coverage. If the county commissioners want to keep social services and public health employees covered under the SHRA, they must explicitly state this intention in the resolution creating the CHSA.

Regardless of whether a county opts to keep CHSA employees under the coverage of the SHRA, all CHSAs are required to comply with the federal merit personnel system standards (found at 5 CFR § 900.603). These federal standards are reflected in the SHRA. When a county wants to remove its CHSA employees from the coverage of the SHRA, the county should first conduct a careful review of its personnel policies, procedures, and ordinances to ensure that they comply with and reflect each of the federal merit personnel standards. Among other things, the relevant federal merit personnel system standards mandate recruitment, selection, and retention of employees based on their ability, knowledge, skills, and performance.[71] The federal standards also require that employees be given fair and equitable treatment without regard to race, color, religion, sex, pregnancy, gender identity, national origin, age (as defined by the Age Discrimination in Employment Act), disability, genetic information, marital status, political affiliation, sexual orientation, status as a parent, or labor-organization affiliation or nonaffiliation.[72]

For more information on the decision to remove CHSA employees from SHRA coverage, please see Kristi Nickodem, *Personnel Decisions for North Carolina's Consolidated Human Services Agencies*, available on the UNC School of Government's website.[73]

Procedural Matters When Forming a New CHSA

Public Hearing

If the BOCC plans to serve as the governing board for a CHSA, it must first hold a public hearing with thirty days' notice to the public, as described earlier in this chapter.[74] The law does not explicitly state that a public hearing is required prior to forming a CHSA with an *appointed* CHS board (as opposed to having the BOCC as the governing board). However, holding such a hearing with appropriate notice is a best practice, given that the creation of a CHSA is a significant change for a county and is likely to draw many questions from county residents and human services employees.

Drafting a Resolution

The law does not explicitly require that counties create a CHSA through the use of a resolution, unless the BOCC is also assuming the powers and duties of the agency governing board. However, it is sensible and prudent for counties to adopt a resolution when forming a CHSA. Among other things, the language of the BOCC resolution forming the CHSA establishes whether employees will be subject to the SHRA or subject solely to county personnel policies. The resolution also establishes and clarifies which county departments or functions are being consolidated into the CHSA. To date, every county in North Carolina that has created a CHSA has done so through a resolution.

Order of Actions

When establishing a new CHSA, the county manager has authority to appoint the agency director, but may do so only with the advice and consent of the governing board.[75] Because of this requirement, there is a logical sequence that should be followed when establishing the CHSA.

1. The BOCC adopts a resolution creating a CHSA.
2. The BOCC appoints a CHS board (based on recommendations from the nominating committee) or directly assumes the powers and duties of the agency governing board through a resolution.
3. The county manager identifies a candidate for CHS director and seeks the advice and consent of the CHSA's governing board.
4. If the CHSA's governing board consents to the appointment, the county manager appoints the CHS director.

Theoretically, these four steps could take place in the same meeting or on the same day, but the order of events is significant under the law. The CHS director cannot be appointed before the CHSA has been created and the governing board is in place because the governing board must consent to the CHS director's appointment.

Timing of the meeting is also important if the BOCC intends to serve as the CHSA's governing board, due to the aforementioned notice and public hearing requirements. The BOCC could hold the hearing, create the CHSA, and assume the powers and duties of the CHSA's governing board in the same meeting, but would have to ensure that the public had at least thirty days' notice of that meeting.

Notes

1. *See* S.L. 2012-126; Chapter 153A, Section 77(b)(3) of the North Carolina General Statutes (hereinafter G.S.).
2. Only Wake County and Mecklenburg County opted to create CHSAs prior to the enactment of S.L. 2012-126.
3. G.S. 153A-77(e).
4. *Compare* G.S. 153A-77(e)(1) *with* G.S. 108A-14(a)(2).
5. G.S. 153A-77(d).
6. G.S. 153A-77(b)(3).
7. G.S. 153A-76(6).
8. As of the publication of this book, no North Carolina counties provide public health services through a public health authority. Hertford County operated a public health authority until dissolving it in June 2018 and joining a district health department (Albemarle Regional Health Services).
9. G.S. 153A-76(5). Cabarrus County operates the only public-hospital authority providing public health services under S.L. 1997-502.
10. G.S. 153A-76(7).
11. Cabarrus County is the sole county with a CHSA that includes social services but not public health.
12. G.S. 153A, § 77(a), (c).
13. G.S. 153A-77(a).
14. *Id.*
15. *Id.*
16. For more information on these BOCC responsibilities related to public health, see Jill Moore, *County Commissioners and Local Boards of Health: What Would Pending Legislation Allow, and What Would It Mean?*, COATES' CANONS: NC LOC. GOV'T L. (blog), June 20, 2012, https://canons.sog.unc.edu/county-commissioners-and-local-boards-of-health-what-would-pending-legislation-allow-and-what-would-it-mean/.
17. The requirement for a health advisory committee applies only to counties that abolish their boards of health after January 1, 2012. This amounts to an exception for Mecklenburg County, which abolished its health boards (a county board of health, and subsequently a CHS board) before that date.
18. This means that the advisory committee must include one physician licensed to practice medicine in North Carolina, one licensed dentist, one licensed optometrist, one licensed veterinarian, one registered nurse, one licensed pharmacist, one county commissioner, one professional engineer, and three representatives of the general public. All members must be residents of the county where the CHSA is located.
19. *See* G.S. 153A-77(a).
20. For more information about public health advisory committees, see Jill Moore, *What Is a County Advisory Committee on Health and Who Has to Have One?*, COATES' CANONS: NC LOC. GOV'T L. (blog), June 21, 2013, https://canons.sog.unc.edu/2013/06/what-is-a-county-advisory-committee-on-health-and-who-has-to-have-one/.
21. Title 10A, Chapter 48B, Sections .1305–.1308 of the North Carolina Administrative Code (hereinafter N.C.A.C.).
22. G.S. 143, art. 33C.
23. G.S. 132.

24. G.S. 153A-77(a), establishing the advisory-committee requirement, only refers to G.S. 130A-35 in the context of membership requirements: "[the board of commissioners] shall appoint an advisory committee consistent with the membership described in G.S. 130A-35." It does not state that the other requirements and provisions applicable to a county board of health apply to an advisory committee.
25. G.S. 153A-77(c).
26. *Id.*
27. A CHS board exercising the powers and duties of an area MH/DD/SA board—which is only permitted for Mecklenburg County—must include *eight* persons who are public advocates, consumers of human services, or family members of the CHSA's clients, including: one person with mental illness, one person with a developmental disability, one person in recovery from substance abuse, one family member of a person with mental illness, one family member of a person with a developmental disability, one family member of a person with a substance abuse problem, and two consumers of other human services. G.S. 153A, § 77(c)(1)–(1a).
28. State law does not squarely address whether board members must continue to maintain their professional qualifications for the duration of their term on the CHS board. Arguably, the answer is yes, since "failure to maintain qualifications for appointment" is one of the grounds for removal of a CHS board member listed in G.S. 153A-77(c).
29. G.S. 153A-77(c).
30. *Id.*
31. By contrast, the statute for boards of health allows county commissioners to appoint a member of the general public when a qualified professional is unavailable to fill the seat. *See* G.S. 130A-35(c).
32. G.S. 153A-77(c).
33. *Id.*
34. *Id.*
35. G.S. 108A-15.1(c)(1); G.S. 153A-77(e)(4).
36. G.S. 153A-77(c).
37. *Id.*
38. *Id.*
39. *Id.*
40. *Id.*
41. G.S. 108A-15.1(b).
42. G.S. 130A-43(b).
43. G.S. 130A, § 39(a)–(f).
44. G.S. 130A, § 24(b)–(d).
45. G.S. 153A-77(d)(5).
46. G.S. 130A-39(g); G.S. 153A-77(d)(1).
47. *See* G.S. 130A, §§ 34.1, 34.4. North Carolina's accreditation rules for local health departments are found in 10A N.C.A.C. 48A.
48. *See* 10A N.C.A.C. 48B, § .1300.
49. *Id.*, § .1303.
50. The current HDSAI Interpretation Document is available on the North Carolina Local Health Department Accreditation Program's website at *Accreditation Documents*, NC Loc. Health Dep't Accreditation, https://nclhdaccreditation.unc.edu/process/documents/#hdsai (last visited March 20, 2023).
51. G.S. 153A-77(d)(2).
52. G.S. 153A-77(d)(8).
53. G.S. 153A-77(d)(3).
54. G.S. 153A-77(d)(1).
55. G.S. 130A-130.

56. G.S. 130A-144(e).
57. G.S. 130A-153(a).
58. G.S. 153A-77(d)(7).
59. G.S. 153A-77(d)(9).
60. G.S. 108A-9(2).
61. G.S. 153A-77(d)(10).
62. G.S. 153A-77(d)(13). Under a former version of the CHSA statute, a CHSA could include the functions of the area MH/DD/SA authority. This language regarding dispute resolution procedures in the CHS board statute is likely intended to reflect the responsibility of area authorities to develop dispute resolution procedures (*see* 10A N.C.A.C 27G, § .0808) but was not omitted or changed when the statute was revised in 2012. Changes made to the law in 2012 now prohibit a BOCC from consolidating an area MH/DD/SA services board into a CHS board (*see* G.S. 153A-76(6)).
63. G.S. 153A-77(e); *compare with* G.S. 108A-12 (DSS board's authority to appoint the DSS director); G.S. 130A-40 (local board of health's authority to appoint the local health director).
64. G.S. 153A-77(e).
65. *Id.*; *compare with* G.S. 108A-14(a)(2) (power of DSS director to appoint staff); G.S. 130A-41(b)(12) (power of local health director to appoint staff).
66. G.S. 153A-77(e). These powers and duties are primarily found in G.S. 108A-14 (DSS director) and G.S. 130A-41 (local health director), though some powers and duties are scattered throughout other portions of the North Carolina General Statutes and the North Carolina Administrative Code.
67. *See* G.S. 130A-6 (regarding delegation of the local health director's powers and duties) and G.S. 108A-14 (regarding delegation of the DSS director's powers and duties).
68. G.S. 153A-77(e). The law does not expressly require the CHS director to delegate local health director powers and duties to the appointee who meets the G.S. 130A-40(a) requirements. There is no equivalent requirement for the CHS director to appoint someone with particular social services experience or qualifications, though many CHS directors will find it necessary and pragmatic to make such an appointment.
69. *See* G.S. 126-5(a)(2).
70. G.S. 153A-77(d).
71. 5 CFR § 900.603(a), (d).
72. *Id.*, § 900.603(e).
73. Kristi Nickodem, *Personnel Decisions for North Carolina's Consolidated Human Services Agencies*, Soc. Servs. L. Bull. No. 49 (UNC School of Government, Dec. 2021), https://www.sog.unc.edu/sites/default/files/reports/SSLB%2049.pdf.
74. G.S. 153A-77(a).
75. G.S. 153A-77(e).

Chapter 17

Regional Social Services Departments and Boards

Since March 2019, North Carolina counties have had authority to voluntarily join together to create regional departments of social services.[1] However, as of the publication of this book, no North Carolina counties have opted to form a regional DSS. This chapter will discuss the structure and authority of a regional social services department, the formation and dissolution of regional departments, the composition and appointment of regional boards for social services, and the appointment of a regional social services director.

Structure and Authority of Regional Departments of Social Services

Like district health departments (which are also composed of multiple counties), a regional DSS is a separate legal entity from the counties involved. Specifically, a regional DSS is a "public authority."[2] This means that a regional DSS is a special-purpose local government entity, subject to many of the same laws that apply to county departments (e.g., laws relating to public records, open meetings, and financial management), but is not a county department or a unit of local government and has no power to levy taxes.[3] A regional DSS would have its own director, governing board, staff, and budget—all separate from the counties that have formed the regional DSS. Neither the regional director nor the director's staff would be county employees.

A regional DSS is required to have centralized administrative operations that are geographically located in one county but must also maintain a physical presence for delivering social services in every county served by the region.[4] State law allows regional social services departments to include more than one judicial district but requires counties to make every effort to include complete judicial districts in a single regional DSS (rather than dividing a judicial district between departments).[5]

Formation and Financing of a Regional Department of Social Services

A regional DSS may be formed upon mutual agreement of each of the county boards of commissioners involved.[6] If a county has a county board of social services or consolidated human services board in place, that board must also agree (along with the county commissioners) for the county to join the formation of the new regional DSS. Likewise, for a county to join an *existing* regional DSS, mutual agreement of all involved boards of county commissioners is required, along with agreement from the county board of social services or consolidated human services board in place in the county seeking to join the regional DSS (if applicable).[7]

A regional social services department may incorporate all social services programs offered by the county departments or it may include only a selected subset of programs and services.[8] For example, a regional DSS could focus exclusively on adult services (such as adult protective services and guardianship), public assistance programs, child welfare services, or child support enforcement.

If the regional DSS does not incorporate *all* social services programs that must be provided by counties, then each county in the region must continue to operate its own department (either a county DSS or a consolidated human services agency, along with its own governing board and director) to offer the mandated programs and services not provided by the regional DSS.

Each county that joins a regional DSS is required to contribute financially to it.[9] Counties that choose to create or join a regional DSS must enter into a written agreement with one another regarding their respective financial responsibilities. Specifically, this agreement must establish the amount or method in which each county will appropriate funds to the department for the administration of social services and public assistance programs, the county share of public assistance programs, and any recoupments following fiscal or program monitoring or audit findings.[10]

Regional Boards of Social Services

The governing board for a regional DSS, known as a regional board of social services, has the same powers and duties as the county social services board with respect to the services or programs that have been assigned to the regional DSS.[11] The regional board must include at least twelve members but may be increased up to eighteen members by agreement of all boards of county commissioners for counties making up the regional DSS.[12]

Appointment Authority

The appointment authority for a regional board of social services is similar to the appointment authority for a county board of social services.

- The board of commissioners of each county in the region appoints two members, one of whom may be a county commissioner.[13] If more than

eight counties join the regional social services department, the board of commissioners of each county in the region appoints only one member to the regional board (who may be a county commissioner).
- The state Social Services Commission appoints two members.
- The seated members of the regional social services board appoint members to fill any remaining vacancies.

The composition of the regional social services board must reasonably reflect the population makeup of the region and provide equitable region-wide representation. All members are required to be residents of the region.[14]

Dissolution and Reappointment of the Board
Whenever a county joins or withdraws from an existing regional social services department, the existing regional board of social services must be dissolved and a new board must be appointed.[15] However, an appointing authority could choose to reappoint a member who was on the previous (dissolved) board, assuming the member is still a resident of the region.

Vacancies on the Board
As with county social services boards, a vacancy on a regional board of social services leaving an unexpired portion of a term must be filled by the appointing authority that appointed the board member who died, resigned, or was removed from the board.[16] For example, if a board member appointed by the Social Services Commission resigns, the Commission is the sole entity with authority to appoint another board member to fill that vacant seat for the remainder of the unexpired term. The term of an individual appointed to fill a vacancy lasts only as long as the unexpired term of the board member who vacated the seat on the board.[17]

Terms and Term Limits
Members of a regional board of social services serve three-year terms.[18] When a regional social services board is first formed, term lengths must be staggered: two of the original members must serve one-year terms, another two original members must serve two-year terms, and the remainder of the original members serve regular three-year terms.[19]

A member may not serve more than three consecutive three-year terms on a regional board of social services.[20]

A county commissioner member may serve on the regional social services board only as long as the member is a county commissioner.[21] This is different from county social services boards, where a county commissioner's term on the board is not tied to or affected by the individual's tenure or term as a county commissioner.

Board Business

Board Chair and Secretary

The regional board of social services must elect a board member to serve as chair on an annual basis. The regional social services director serves as secretary to the board.[22]

Quorum

A majority of the actual membership, excluding vacancies, constitutes a quorum for purposes of conducting business as a board.[23]

Meetings

The regional board of social services must meet at least quarterly. The board chair or three of the board members may call a special meeting.[24]

Per Diem

Board members may receive a per diem in an amount established by the county commissioner members of the regional board. The county commissioner members also have authority to set a policy for reimbursement of board members for subsistence and travel.[25]

Attorney

A regional board of social services is authorized to contract for the services of an attorney to represent the board, the regional social services department, and its employees, as appropriate.[26]

Removal of a Board Member

Authority to remove a board member from an appointed county board of social services rests with the entity that appointed the board member (see Chapter 5). However, state law vests all authority to remove a regional social services board member in the regional board of social services *itself*.[27]

After giving a board member written notice and an opportunity to respond, the regional board of social services may remove the board member if the member has

1. committed a felony or other crime involving moral turpitude;
2. violated a state law governing conflicts of interest;
3. violated a written policy adopted by the county board of commissioners of each county in the region;
4. habitually failed to attend meetings; or
5. engaged in conduct that tends to bring the office into disrepute.[28]

Liability Insurance

A regional board of social services is authorized to provide liability insurance for the members of the board and the employees of the regional social services department (including the director).[29] The purchase of liability insurance waives both the regional board of social services' and the regional social services department's governmental immunity, to the extent of insurance coverage, for any act or omission occurring in the exercise of a governmental function.[30] For more discussion on the impact of insurance coverage on governmental immunity, please see Chapter 15 of this book.

Appointment of the Regional Social Services Director

The regional social services board has sole authority to appoint the regional social services director.[31] The regional social services director has all the powers and duties of a county director of social services (see Chapter 7) with respect to the services or programs that have been assigned to the regional DSS.[32] This includes the authority to hire and supervise staff of the regional DSS. The director also has authority to enter into other contracts on behalf of the regional DSS in accordance with the Local Government Finance Act.[33]

Dissolution of a Regional DSS

If the board of commissioners of each county in the region determines that the regional social services department is not operating in the best interests of the respective counties, they may direct that the department be dissolved.[34] Likewise, a county may withdraw from the regional DSS if its board of commissioners determines that the department is not operating in the best interests of that county.[35] NCDHHS must be notified in writing before a regional DSS is dissolved.[36]

As described above, whenever a county joins or withdraws from an existing regional social services department, the regional board of social services must be dissolved and a new board must be appointed.[37]

Dissolution or withdrawal will only be effective at the end of the fiscal year in which it occurred.[38] State law establishes procedures for distributing budgetary surplus available to a regional social services department to counties after a dissolution or withdrawal occurs.[39]

Notes

1. Chapter 108A, Section 15.7 of the North Carolina General Statutes (hereinafter G.S.). This change in the law was enacted in Session Law 2017-41, § 4.1.
2. G.S. 108A-15.7(g); G.S. 159-7(b)(10).
3. For more information about special-purpose local governments and public authorities, see Kara Millonzi, *Special Purpose Local Governments and Public Authorities*, COATES' CANONS: NC LOC. GOV'T L. (blog) (Feb. 10, 2015), https://canons.sog.unc.edu/2015/02/special-purpose-local-governments-and-public-authorities/.
4. G.S. 108A-15.7(a).
5. G.S. 108A-15.7(d).
6. G.S. 108A-15.7(a).
7. G.S. 108A-15.7(c).
8. G.S. 108A-15.7(b).
9. G.S. 108A-15.7(f).
10. Title 10A, Chapter 67A, Section .0301 of the North Carolina Administrative Code.
11. G.S. 108A-15.8(a).
12. G.S. 108A-15.8(b). This agreement to increase the size of the board must be evidenced by concurrent resolutions adopted by the affected boards of county commissioners.
13. G.S. 108A-15.8(c).
14. *Id.*
15. G.S. 108A-15.8(e).
16. G.S. 108A-15.8(f).
17. *Id.*
18. G.S. 108A-15.8(d).
19. *Id.*
20. *Id.*
21. *Id.*
22. G.S. 108A-15.8(g).
23. G.S. 108A-15.8(h).
24. G.S. 108A-15.8(k).
25. G.S. 108A-15.8(j).
26. G.S. 108A-15.8(l).
27. G.S. 108A-15.8(i).
28. *Id.*
29. G.S. 108A-15.8(l).
30. *Id.*
31. G.S. 108A, § 15.8(a), .10.
32. G.S. 108A-15.10.
33. *Id.*
34. G.S. 108A-15.9(a).
35. G.S. 108A-15.9(b).
36. G.S. 108A-15.9(d).
37. G.S. 108A-15.8(e).
38. G.S. 108A-15.9(c).
39. G.S. 108A-15.9(e).

Appendix A

Comparisons of Local Social Services Boards

Table A.1. Types of Local Governing Boards for Social Services

Board	Organization	Board Members Selected By[a]	Director Appointed By
County board of social services	County DSS	Appointment (3 or 5)	Board
BOCC as board of social services	County DSS	Election	BOCC
CHS board	CHSA	Appointment (Up to 25)	County manager, with the advice and consent of the CHS board
BOCC as CHS board[b]	CHSA	Election	County manager, with the advice and consent of the BOCC
Regional board of social services	Regional DSS (multicounty)	Appointment (12–18)	Board

Note: BOCC = board of county commissioners; CHS = consolidated human services, CHSA = consolidated human services agency.

[a] Numbers in parentheses represent the number of members on each appointed board.

[b] An advisory committee for public health must be appointed if the CHSA includes public health. G.S. 153A-77(a). There is no corresponding requirement to appoint an advisory committee for social services, though the BOCC may choose to do so.

Table A.2. Selected Powers and Duties of Local Social Services Boards

	County Board of Social Services	CHS Board	Regional Board of Social Services
Appoint agency director	Yes	No, county manager appoints director with the advice and consent of the CHS board.	Yes
Help director to prepare and recommend the agency budget	Yes, along with director	Yes[a]	Yes, though BOCCs establish the amount or method for county funding of the department.[b]
Review certain confidential social services records	Yes	Yes	Yes
Consult with director about problems affecting the agency	Yes	Yes	Yes
Advise local officials	Yes	Yes, through the county manager.	Yes
Adopt local public health rules	No	Yes[c]	No
Adjudicate appeals related to local public rules or fines imposed by the local health director	No	Yes[c]	No
Impose fees for public health services	No	Yes[c] (subject to BOCC approval)	No
Develop dispute resolution procedures for contractors and clients	No	Yes	No
Enter into contracts for legal services without BOCC approval	No[d]	No[d]	Yes
Purchase liability insurance	No[e]	No[e]	Yes

Note: BOCC = board of county commissioners; CHS = consolidated human services.

[a] The CHS board plans and recommends the agency's budget (G.S. 153A-77(d)(7)) but is prohibited from transmitting or presenting the budget for local health programs (G.S. 130A-43(b)(2)) and does not approve the final budget.

[b] It is the BOCCs for each county in the region—not the regional board of social services—that must agree upon the amount or method in which each county will appropriate funds to the department for the administration of social services and public assistance programs, the county share of public assistance programs, and any recoupments following fiscal or program monitoring or audit findings (Title 10A, Chapter 67A, Section .0301 of the North Carolina Administrative Code).

[c] The CHS board has this authority only if the consolidated human services agency includes public health.

[d] If a BOCC has assumed the powers and duties of a social services board or CHS board, the BOCC has authority to contract with an attorney.

[e] If a BOCC has assumed the powers and duties of a social services board or CHS board, the BOCC has authority to purchase liability insurance.

Table A.3. Social Services Board Member Term Length and Term Limit

Board	Regular Term Length	Term Limit[a]	County Commissioner's Term on Board Contemporaneous with Term on BOCC?
County board of social services[b]	3 years	2 consecutive terms	No
CHS board[b]	4 years[c]	2 consecutive terms	Yes
Regional board of social services[b]	3 years[d]	3 consecutive terms	Yes
BOCC (assuming powers and duties of board of social services or CHS board)	Coincides with term as county commissioner	No limit	Yes

Note: BOCC = board of county commissioners; CHS = consolidated human services.

[a] The maximum number of consecutive terms that a board member may hold.

[b] Board members selected by appointment.

[c] When a CHS board is first formed, members may be appointed for less than a four-year term in order to establish a uniform staggered-term structure for the board. G.S. 153A-77(c).

[d] When a regional social services board is first formed, term lengths must be staggered: Two of the original members must serve one-year terms, another two original members must serve two-year terms, and the remainder of the original members serve regular three-year terms. G.S. 108A-15.8(d).

Table A.4. Appointment of Social Services Board Members

Board Type (No. of Members)	Appointing Authority		Board Members Appointed by BOCC and SSC
	BOCC	SSC	
County social services (3 or 5)	Appoints 1 member on a 3-member board or 2 members on a 5-member board	Appoints 1 member on a 3-member board or 2 members on a 5-member board	Appoint 1 member
CHS (up to 25)	Appoints all members from a slate of nominees presented by the CHS board[a]		
Regional social services (12–18)	BOCC of each county involved appoints 2 members[b]	Appoints 2 members	Appoint members to fill all remaining vacancies on the board

Note: BOCC = board of county commissioners; SSC = Social Services Commission; CHS = consolidated human services.

[a] When a CHS board is first formed, the BOCC must create a nominating committee composed of members of the current (preconsolidation) board of health and social services board, as well as the board responsible for managing mental health, developmental disabilities, and substance abuse services in the county. The nominating committee recommends members for the new CHS board and the BOCC must make appointments based upon those recommendations.

[b] If more than eight counties join the regional department, each BOCC appoints only one member.

Appendix B

Selected Resources for Social Services Board Members

For the most up-to-date resources that may be relevant to social services boards, please visit the **North Carolina Human Services Hub** at https://humanservices.sog .unc.edu/. Selected additional resources that may be helpful to social services board members are listed by topic below. All web addresses are current as of April 2023.

Consolidated Human Services Agencies

Kristi A. Nickodem, *Personnel Decisions for North Carolina's Consolidated Human Services Agencies,* Social Services Bulletin 49 (UNC School of Government, December 2021), https://www.sog.unc.edu/publications/bulletins/ personnel-decisions-north-carolinas-consolidated-human-services-agencies.

Ethics

A. Fleming Bell, II, *Ethics, Conflicts, and Offices: A Guide for Local Officials*, 2nd ed. (UNC School of Government, 2010).

Frayda S. Bluestein and Norma R. Houston, "Ethics and Conflicts of Interest," chap. 7 in *County and Municipal Government in North Carolina*, 2nd ed., edited by Frayda S. Bluestein (UNC School of Government, 2014).

Hiring and Evaluating the Director

Diane M. Juffras, *Recruitment and Selection Law for Local Government Employers* (UNC School of Government, 2013).

U.S. Equal Employment Opportunity Commission's guidance on "Prohibited Employment Policies/Practices," https://www.eeoc.gov/prohibited -employment-policiespractices.

Vaughn Mamlin Upshaw, *How Are We Doing? Evaluating Manager and Board Performance* (UNC School of Government 2014).

Vaughn Mamlin Upshaw, John A. Rible IV, and Carl W. Stenberg, *Getting the Right Fit: The Governing Board's Role in Hiring a Manager* (UNC School of Government, 2011).

Note: *How Are We Doing* and *Getting the Right Fit* discuss hiring and evaluating a county manager, but some of the concepts may be useful for recruiting and evaluating the social services director.

Liability

Trey Allen, *Local Government Immunity to Lawsuits in North Carolina* (UNC School of Government, 2018).

Anthony J. Baker, "Civil Liability of the Local Government and Its Officials and Employees," chap. 6 in *County and Municipal Government in North Carolina*, 2nd ed., edited by Frayda S. Bluestein (UNC School of Government, 2014).

Open Meetings

Trey Allen, *'Full and Accurate' Minutes: A Primer*, Local Government Law Bulletin 140 (UNC School of Government, January 2019), https://www.sog.unc.edu/publications/bulletins/full-and-accurate-minutes-primer.

Frayda S. Bluestein and David M. Lawrence, *Open Meetings and Local Governments in North Carolina: Some Questions and Answers*, 8th ed. (UNC School of Government, 2017).

Frayda S. Bluestein, "Open Meetings and Other Legal Requirements for Local Government Boards," chap. 9 in *County and Municipal Government in North Carolina*, 2nd ed., edited by Frayda S. Bluestein (UNC School of Government, 2014).

Public Records

Frayda S. Bluestein, "Public Records," chap. 8 in *County and Municipal Government in North Carolina*, 2nd ed., edited by Frayda S. Bluestein (UNC School of Government, 2014).

David M. Lawrence, *Public Records Law for North Carolina Local Governments*, 2nd ed. (UNC School of Government, 2009).

Records Retention

"Local Government Agencies," State Archives of North Carolina, North Carolina Department of Natural and Cultural Resources, https://archives.ncdcr.gov/government/local.

Rules of Procedure

Trey Allen and A. Fleming Bell, II, *Suggested Procedural Rules for Local Appointed Boards* (UNC School of Government, 2020).

Social Services

John L. Saxon, *Social Services in North Carolina* (UNC School of Government, 2008).

Aimee N. Wall, "Social Services," chap. 39 in *County and Municipal Government in North Carolina*, 2nd ed., edited by Frayda S. Bluestein (UNC School of Government, 2014).

North Carolina Association of County Boards of Social Services (web site), http://www.ncacbss.org/.

Coates' Canons Selected Posts

Coates' Canons (https://canons.sog.unc.edu/) is a UNC School of Government blog featuring blog posts from School of Government faculty regarding legal issues affecting local governments and other public agencies in North Carolina. The list below is a small sampling of hundreds of posts that may be useful to social services directors and board members. Individuals can subscribe to the blog, search posts by keyword, and browse posts by topic.

Posts by Frayda Bluestein

"Retention Schedules for Local Governments: Five Things You Should Know," May 16, 2019, https://canons.sog.unc.edu/2019/05/retention-schedules-for-local-governments-five-things-you-should-know/.

"How to Approve Minutes and General Accounts of Closed Sessions," June 5, 2018, https://canons.sog.unc.edu /2018/06/how-to-approve-minutes-and-general-accounts-of-closed-sessions/.

"Setting Salaries and Closed Sessions," December 17, 2015, https://canons.sog.unc.edu/2015/12/setting-salaries-and-closed-sessions/.

"Quick Reference Guide for Closed Sessions," March 13, 2014, https://canons.sog.unc.edu/2014/03/quick-reference-guide-for-closed-session-meetings/.

Posts by Aimee Wall

"Access to Confidential Client Records by Social Services Governing Boards," April 26, 2016, https://canons.sog.unc.edu/2016/04/access-confidential-records-social-services-governing-boards/.

"Boards of Social Services and Fraud Investigations," April 18, 2012, https://canons.sog.unc.edu/2012/04/boards-of-social-services-and-fraud-investigations/.